Better Homes and Gardens®

ENCYCLOPEDIA
of
COOKING

Volume 16

Easy Italian Dressing, Tomato Soup Dressing, and fluffy Lemonade Dressing are only a few of the delicious homemade salad dressings that you'll proudly serve as highlights of the meal.

On the cover: Whether it's by the link and accompanied with potato salad or sliced for a sandwich, sausage is an all-time favorite. Popular accompaniments are mustard and pickles.

BETTER HOMES AND GARDENS BOOKS
NEW YORK • DES MOINES

© Meredith Corporation, 1970, 1971, 1973. All Rights Reserved.
Printed in the United States of America.
Special Edition. First Printing.
Library of Congress Catalog Card Number: 73-83173
SBN: 696-02036-X

SALAD DRESSING

Valuable hints on how to prepare and use these essential partners for salad.

Most people agree that a salad without dressing is lacking something—it's nice, perhaps, but not perfect. In saladmaking, the mixture of ingredients called the dressing serves two functions: it adds flavor to the salad and it binds the ingredients together, sometimes literally and sometimes by flavor accent only.

Quite naturally, the history of salad dressings is linked with the history of salad. In fact, like salad, salad dressings can be traced as far back as the ancient Greeks and Romans. Unlike most of the salad dressings of today, which contain several ingredients, the first definable salad dressing used by these people consisted of only one ingredient—salt.

The classic mixture of oil and vinegar is a dressing of long standing. In fact, a mixture of greens and sometimes other vegetables dressed with oil and vinegar was the only type of salad known in European countries several centuries ago.

By the 1700s, however, many chefs were becoming more experimental, and salad dressings were one of the things that received attention. Mayonnaise, a sauce that is considered as much of a classic dressing as oil and vinegar, was one of the developments of this time. Apparently, however, there were still rules on what constituted a good salad dressing because it is recorded that one of the French chefs of that time reprimanded Marie Antoinette for using an incorrect dressing.

Another milestone in the history of salad dressing occurred in the 1920s when prepared salad dressings were first sold. Since then, the variety of prepared dressings available has increased continually. Today, homemakers have the choice of dressing salads with a homemade salad dressing or one of the dozens of dressing mixes they can prepare at home (usually with vinegar and oil) and bottled dressings which are available. Now, homemakers even have a choice of low-calorie versions in many of the mixes and bottled dressings.

How to complement salads

When adding a salad dressing to a salad, one of the most important things to remember is to use salad dressing with discretion. If you use too little dressing, the salad loses character. On the other hand, if you use too much dressing, you are likely to drown the basic salad flavor.

However, this reminder does not answer the question of what dressing goes with what salad. Although there are several standard combinations, such as French dressing or vinegar and oil dressing on tossed salads, poppy seed or celery seed dressing on fresh fruit salads, and mayonnaise on meat salads or potato salads, don't limit yourself to these. Start experimenting with new flavor combinations, such as French dressing on fruit salads, and also with new salad dressings.

Your personal preferences and those of your family and guests are one of the most important guides to use when matching salads and dressings—if it has an appealing appearance and flavor, it is a good combination. As a starting place for finding out what combinations you like, use the following general hints.

One thing that helps you to determine which dressing to use is whether the salad is an appetizer, side dish, main dish, or dessert salad. Since the purpose of an appetizer salad is to whet the appetite, the dressing must help to accomplish this. Therefore, use a light dressing rather than a heavy dressing and a tart, spicy dressing rather than a sweet dressing on first-course salads. Dressings such as an oil-vinegar dressing and fruit juices fulfill these requirements.

The dressing for a side dish or main dish salad can range from light to heavy and from mild to highly seasoned, depending on the ingredients in the salad. Dressings for dessert salads are usually quite sweet, although they are sometimes flavored with a rather tart fruit juice.

The ingredients in the salad are another important guide when matching salads and salad dressings. Although flavor is probably the main consideration, also make sure that the texture and color of the salad dressing complement the salad.

The type of dressing you choose depends on what flavor you want to be dominant—the salad or the dressing. For example, a wedge of lettuce doesn't have much flavor by itself, so you can serve a dressing with a prominent flavor such as blue cheese dressing or a highly seasoned French dressing with it. However, if you are serving a deluxe tossed salad that includes several types of salad greens, red cabbage, shredded carrots, and other vegetables, put the emphasis on the salad flavor by using a simple dressing such as oil and vinegar or a basic French dressing. The following box gives some more guides on which dressing to use.

Dressing tips

French dressings cling readily to greens and are great for marinating vegetables. The tart-sweet ones add tang to fruit salads.

Cooked dressings add luscious appeal to potato salads. Sweet cooked dressings are especially good as fruit toppings.

Cheese-flavored dressings used with vegetables, make exciting companions.

Sour cream dressings add zip to fruit and vegetable salads. They're also delightful with main dish salad bowls.

Mayonnaise and salad dressing, with their varied combinations, heighten the flavor of meat, seafood, egg, and molded salads. When combined with whipped cream, mayonnaise is excellent on fruit salads.

How to prepare

Mixing a salad dressing can be as simple as shaking together several ingredients, or it can be a more complicated process that involves cooking or extended beating. But no matter what the preparation technique, the objective is to prepare a flavorful, enticing dressing. Numerous combinations of ingredients will fulfill this objective, but generally salad dressings are divided into four types—cooked, dairy, oil-based, and mayonnaise-based.

Cooked: This type of salad dressing is thickened with eggs (at least the yolks) and/or starch or a cooked syrup. Besides the thickening agent, cooked dressings usually include sugar, vinegar or another acid ingredient, and seasonings.

When making a cooked salad dressing, remember to follow directions. Specifically, pay careful attention to the length of cooking time and the adding of the eggs to the hot mixture (first, stir a little hot mixture into the eggs and then stir this into the remaining hot mixture).

The commercial product, salad dressing, fits into this category. Although this product is often substituted for mayonnaise, it doesn't have as much oil.

Fruit Dip Fluff

½ cup sugar
⅓ cup light corn syrup
¼ cup hot water
1 stiffly beaten egg white
   Dash salt
   Few drops vanilla
½ cup mayonnaise
1½ teaspoons shredded orange peel

In small saucepan combine sugar, light corn syrup, and hot water. Heat slowly, stirring till all sugar is dissolved. Then, boil without stirring till mixture reaches soft-ball stage (236°). Gradually beat hot syrup into stiffly beaten egg white. Add salt and vanilla. Cool mixture thoroughly.

Fold mayonnaise and shredded orange peel into cooled mixture; chill thoroughly. Serve as dressing on fruit salad. Makes 1⅔ cups.

Cooked Dressing

- 2 tablespoons all-purpose flour
- 2 tablespoons sugar
- 1 teaspoon dry mustard
  Dash cayenne
- 2 slightly beaten egg yolks
- 3/4 cup milk
- 1/4 cup vinegar
- 1 1/2 teaspoons butter

Mix together flour, sugar, mustard, 1/2 teaspoon salt, and cayenne in small saucepan. Add egg yolks and milk; cook, stirring constantly, over low heat till thick. Add vinegar and butter; mix. Cool thoroughly. Makes 1 cup.

Lemonade Dressing

- 1 6-ounce can lemonade concentrate
- 2 beaten eggs
- 1/3 cup sugar
- 1 cup whipping cream

Thaw concentrate. In small saucepan combine eggs, lemonade concentrate, and sugar. Cook and stir over low heat till thickened. Cool. Whip cream; fold in. Chill thoroughly. Serve with fruit salads. Makes 3 cups dressing.

Dairy: Many salad dressings have dairy products as their main ingredient: Whipped cream, cream cheese, sour cream, yogurt, or cottage cheese combined with seasonings.

Dairy dressings are easy to prepare. Usually, it requires only a few minutes to stir the dressing ingredients together. However, as with most salad dressings, you should prepare dairy dressings several hours before serving to allow the flavors to blend while the dressing chills.

Berry-Sour Cream Dressing

- 1 cup dairy sour cream
- 1/2 10-ounce package frozen, sliced strawberries, thawed (1/2 cup)

Blend sour cream and fruit. Chill. Serve with fruit salads. Makes about 1 1/4 cups.

Mushroom Dressing

- 1 3-ounce can chopped mushrooms, drained
- 1 cup dairy sour cream
- 1/3 cup mayonnaise or salad dressing
- 2 tablespoons well-drained pickle relish
- 2 tablespoons milk
- 3/4 teaspoon salt
- 1/2 teaspoon Worcestershire sauce

Chop any large pieces of mushrooms. Combine with sour cream, mayonnaise, pickle relish, milk, salt, and Worcestershire sauce; chill thoroughly. Serve with lettuce wedges or vegetable salads. Makes 2 cups dressing.

Western Blue Cheese Dressing

In pint-sized screw-top jar combine 2 ounces blue cheese, crumbled (1/2 cup), and 3/4 cup dairy sour cream; stir in 2 tablespoons milk. Add 1 tablespoon salad oil, dash Worcestershire sauce, 2 teaspoons grated Parmesan cheese, dash onion salt, dash garlic salt, and dash pepper; mix well. Add 3 tablespoons white wine vinegar; cover jar and shake well. Chill. Serve over tossed green salads. Makes 1 2/3 cups.

Sweet-Sour Dressing

- 1 cup dairy sour cream
- 2 tablespoons white vinegar
- 2 tablespoons sugar
- 1/2 teaspoon salt

Combine sour cream and white vinegar. Stir in sugar and salt. Chill thoroughly. Toss with shredded cabbage. Makes 1 cup dressing.

Nippy Nectar Dressing

In small mixing bowl beat together one 3-ounce package cream cheese, softened; 2 tablespoons honey; 1 teaspoon grated lemon peel; 1 tablespoon lemon juice; and 1/8 teaspoon salt. Gradually add 1/2 cup salad oil, beating till mixture is thickened. Chill thoroughly. Serve with fruit salads. Makes about 1 cup dressing.

Horseradish Dressing

½ cup dairy sour cream
¼ cup mayonnaise or salad
    dressing
 1 tablespoon prepared horseradish
 1 teaspoon sugar
¼ teaspoon salt
 2 drops bottled hot pepper sauce
 2 drops Worcestershire sauce

Combine sour cream, mayonnaise, horseradish, sugar, salt, hot pepper sauce, and Worcestershire sauce; chill thoroughly. Serve with meat or seafood salads. Makes 2 cups.

Crunchy Cream Dressing

Tiny vegetable pieces add crunch—

½ cup finely chopped, unpeeled
    cucumber
 2 tablespoons finely chopped
    green pepper
 2 tablespoons finely chopped
    green onion
 2 tablespoons thinly sliced
    radishes
    • • •
 1 cup dairy sour cream
½ teaspoon salt
    Dash pepper

Combine cucumber, green pepper, onion, and radishes. Stir in sour cream, salt, and pepper; mix well. Chill thoroughly. Serve over lettuce or cabbage salads. Makes 1½ cups.

Banana-Cheese Dressing

 1 3-ounce package cream cheese,
    softened
 2 tablespoons milk
 1 fully ripe banana
 1 tablespoon sugar
 1 tablespoon lemon juice
    Dash salt

Blend softened cream cheese with milk. Mash banana; add sugar, lemon juice, and dash salt. Stir the banana mixture into cheese mixture. Serve with fruit salads. Makes 1 cup.

Dairy-Fruit Dressing

½ cup dairy sour cream
 1 tablespoon honey
 1 teaspoon lemon juice
¼ teaspoon salt

Combine sour cream, honey, lemon juice, and salt. Chill. Serve with sweetened or canned fruit. Makes about ½ cup dressing.

Tarragon Dressing

 1 cup dairy sour cream
½ cup mayonnaise
 1 teaspoon vinegar
½ teaspoon dried tarragon
    leaves, crushed
¼ teaspoon seasoned salt

Combine sour cream, mayonnaise, vinegar, tarragon, and seasoned salt. Chill. Serve with seafood or vegetable salads. Makes 1½ cups.

Rosy Salad Dressing

 1 8-ounce package cream cheese,
    softened
 1 cup dairy sour cream
¾ cup cranberry relish

Combine softened cream cheese and dairy sour cream; beat till smooth. Stir in cranberry relish. Chill at least 2 hours. Serve with fruit salads. Makes about 3 cups dressing.

Chef's Cheese Dressing

 3 ounces blue cheese,
    crumbled (¾ cup)
½ cup olive *or* salad oil
 2 tablespoons white vinegar
 1 tablespoon lemon juice
 1 teaspoon anchovy paste
½ clove garlic, minced
    Salt and pepper

Thoroughly combine blue cheese, olive *or* salad oil, white vinegar, lemon juice, anchovy paste, and garlic. Season with salt and pepper. Chill thoroughly. Stir before serving. Makes 1 cup.

Oil-based: The classic oil and vinegar dressing (usually three parts oil to one part vinegar), French dressing, and mayonnaise are all oil-based salad dressings (see *French Salad Dressing* and *Mayonnaise* for recipes). However, many variations of these classic recipes as well as numerous other dressings for fruit and vegetable salads also have oil as a base.

Most oil-based dressings are easy to prepare since mixing the ingredients is all that's required. The easiest way to mix a dressing of this type other than mayonnaise is in a screw-top jar. Simply measure the ingredients into the jar, screw the lid on tightly, and shake vigorously. However, as the dressing sets, the oil and other ingredients separate, so shake the dressing again just before using it.

Zippy Emerald Dressing

    1 cup salad oil
 1/3 cup vinegar
 1/4 cup chopped onion
 1/4 cup snipped parsley
    2 tablespoons finely chopped
        green pepper
    2 teaspoons sugar
1 1/2 teaspoons dry mustard
 1/2 teaspoon salt
 1/8 teaspoon cayenne

Combine salad oil, vinegar, onion, parsley, green pepper, sugar, dry mustard, salt, and cayenne in screw-top jar. Cover; let stand at room temperature for about 1 hour. Shake to blend thoroughly. Serve with seafood or tossed green salads. Makes about 1 1/2 cups.

As the perfect finishing touch for a fruit-filled, molded gelatin salad as well as for other fresh or canned fruit salads generously spoon on rich, creamy Banana-Cheese Dressing.

Glossy Fruit Dressing

½ cup sugar
¼ cup vinegar
1 teaspoon celery salt
1 teaspoon paprika
1 teaspoon dry mustard
½ teaspoon salt
½ teaspoon grated onion
1 cup salad oil

In small saucepan combine sugar and vinegar; heat and stir just till sugar is dissolved. Cool. Add celery salt, paprika, mustard, salt, and onion. Add oil in slow stream, beating with an electric mixer or a rotary beater till dressing is thick. Makes 1½ cups.

Fruit French Dressing

1 cup salad oil
¼ cup orange juice
3 tablespoons lemon juice
1 tablespoon vinegar
⅓ cup sugar
1 teaspoon salt
1 teaspoon paprika
1 teaspoon grated onion

Mix salad oil, orange juice, lemon juice, vinegar, sugar, salt, paprika, and onion in screw-top jar; cover and shake vigorously. Chill. Shake before serving. Makes about 1⅔ cups.

Shawano Dressing

½ cup salad oil
⅓ cup sugar
⅓ cup catsup
¼ cup vinegar
1 teaspoon salt
1 teaspoon paprika
½ teaspoon dry mustard
2 teaspoons grated onion
1½ teaspoons bottled steak sauce
1 clove garlic, minced

In bowl combine salad oil, sugar, catsup, vinegar, salt, paprika, dry mustard, grated onion, bottled steak sauce, and minced garlic. Blend mixture thoroughly with a beater. Serve with fruit. Makes about 1⅓ cups dressing.

Tomato Soup Dressing

1 10¾-ounce can condensed
    tomato soup
1 cup vinegar
½ cup salad oil
1½ teaspoons Worcestershire sauce
2 tablespoons sugar
1 tablespoon grated onion
2 teaspoons dry mustard
½ teaspoon paprika
¼ teaspoon garlic powder
    Dash cayenne

In screw-top jar combine tomato soup, vinegar, salad oil, and Worcestershire sauce. Add sugar, grated onion, dry mustard, 1½ teaspoons salt, paprika, garlic powder, and cayenne. Cover; shake. Chill thoroughly. Makes 2¼ cups.

Celery Seed Dressing

½ cup sugar
⅓ cup lemon juice
1 teaspoon celery seed
1 teaspoon dry mustard
1 teaspoon paprika
¾ cup salad oil

Combine sugar, lemon juice, celery seed, dry mustard, paprika, and ½ teaspoon salt. Slowly add oil, beating with electric or rotary beater till thick. Makes 1⅓ cups dressing.

Italian Dressing

1 cup salad oil
¼ cup vinegar
1 clove garlic, minced
1 teaspoon salt
½ teaspoon white pepper
½ teaspoon celery salt
¼ teaspoon cayenne
¼ teaspoon dry mustard
    Dash bottled hot pepper sauce

Combine salad oil, vinegar, garlic, salt, white pepper, celery salt, cayenne, dry mustard, and hot pepper sauce in screw-top jar. Cover and shake well. Chill mixture thoroughly. Shake again just before serving. Serve with vegetable salads. Makes 1¼ cups dressing.

Dressing dictionary

French Dressing: Both clear and creamy French dressings are a mixture of oil, vinegar or lemon juice, and seasonings. Clear dressings separate and must be shaken well before using. Creamy dressings are homogenized; thus, they do not separate.

Mayonnaise: This creamy dressing is made by beating oil very slowly into egg, vinegar or lemon juice, and seasonings. The egg emulsifies and prevents separation.

Salad Dressing: Oil and egg are used in lower proportions than in mayonnaise. Starch pastes may be used as thickening agents, as also emulsifiers. The flavor is more tangy than mayonnaise.

Cooked Dressing: Also called boiled dressing, this type is high in egg and low in fat. It is made by cooking a white sauce-egg base to which vinegar, butter or margarine, and seasonings are added.

Sesame Dressing

Toasted sesame seeds give crunch—

Combine ⅔ cup sugar, and ⅓ cup vinegar; blend in 2 tablespoons finely chopped onion, ½ teaspoon salt, ½ teaspoon Worcestershire sauce, ¼ teaspoon dry mustard, ¼ teaspoon paprika, and 4 to 5 drops bottled hot pepper sauce. Gradually add 1 cup salad oil, beating constantly with rotary beater or electric mixer till thick; chill. Stir in 2 to 3 tablespoons toasted sesame seed just before serving. Serve with fruit salads. Makes 1¾ cups.

Snappy Garlic Dressing

In screw-top jar combine ⅔ cup salad oil; ¼ cup vinegar; 1 small clove garlic, minced, 1 teaspoon sugar; ¾ teaspoon salt; ¾ teaspoon dry mustard; and dash freshly ground pepper. Cover and chill several hours. Shake well before serving with salad greens or shredded cabbage. Makes 1 cup dressing.

Mayonnaise-based: As expected, the main ingredient in this type of salad dressing is mayonnaise. Although mayonnaise alone is used as a dressing for some kinds of salads, the addition of other ingredients not only varies the flavor but also increases the versatility.

Preparing mayonnaise-based dressings simply requires blending the ingredients together. Sometimes, however, the blending of ingredients is done in two steps. First, the mayonnaise and seasonings are mixed and then a fluffy ingredient such as whipped cream is folded in. The dressing is chilled before serving.

Apricot Dressing

⅓ cup mayonnaise or salad
    dressing
⅓ cup apricot preserves
½ cup whipping cream

Blend together mayonnaise or salad dressing and apricot preserves. Whip cream till soft peaks form; gently fold into apricot mixture. Serve with fruit salads. Makes 1⅓ cups.

Parmesan Dressing

1 cup mayonnaise
1 tablespoon anchovy paste
½ envelope Parmesan salad dressing mix (1 tablespoon)
¼ cup water
2 tablespoons vinegar

In small mixing bowl combine mayonnaise and anchovy paste. Stir in Parmesan salad dressing mix, water, and vinegar. Serve with vegetable salads. Makes 1½ cups dressing.

Red Currant Dressing

½ cup currant jelly
¼ cup mayonnaise
¼ cup whipping cream

With rotary beater, beat currant jelly till soft and smooth. Blend in mayonnaise. Whip cream; fold into mixture. Makes about 1 cup.

Peanut–Mallow Dressing

½ 7-ounce jar marshmallow creme
¼ cup orange juice

• • •

½ cup peanut butter
¼ cup mayonnaise or salad dressing
1 tablespoon lemon juice

Combine marshmallow creme and orange juice; whip till very fluffy with electric beater. Blend peanut butter, mayonnaise, and lemon juice; fold into marshmallow mixture. Serve over fresh or canned fruit. Makes 2 cups.

Honey Mayonnaise

Blend ½ cup mayonnaise, 2 tablespoons honey, 1 tablespoon lemon juice, ½ teaspoon celery seed, and ¼ teaspoon paprika. Serve with fruit salads. Makes about ¾ cup dressing.

Cream Goddess Dressing

Combine 1 cup mayonnaise, ½ cup dairy sour cream, ⅓ cup snipped parsley, 3 tablespoons snipped chives, 3 tablespoons anchovy paste, 3 tablespoons tarragon vinegar, 1 tablespoon lemon juice, and dash freshly ground pepper. Chill. Serve with salad greens. Makes 2 cups.

Blue Cheese Mayonnaise

In mixing bowl combine 2 tablespoons crumbled blue cheese, softened, and ½ cup mayonnaise. Beat till smooth. Stir in 4 teaspoons milk and few drops bottled hot pepper sauce. Serve with salad greens. If desired, crumble extra blue cheese over top. Makes ½ cup.

Uses

While the most common use for salad dressings is on salads, these flavorful mixtures have several other uses. It is easy to make one kind of salad dressing or another an ingredient in the menu.

Dressings such as mayonnaise, French dressing, and the thick, creamy mixture sold as salad dressing are especially tasty spread on sandwiches, used as a binder for sandwich fillings, or used in appetizer dips or spreads. Steaks and roasts as well as fish and seafood are particularly flavorful when marinated in a highly herbed salad dressing before cooking. And broiled or barbecued meat is tasty when brushed during cooking with a tangy salad dressing.

In addition to homemade salad dressings, you can choose from the wide selection of prepared dressings and dressing mixes (mixed at home with oil or mayonnaise) that are available in the supermarket. Using prepared dressings cuts down the preparation time of salads and other dishes that use salad dressing.

Liver with Mushrooms

A low-calorie main dish—

> 1 4-ounce can sliced mush-
>   rooms, drained
> 1/3 cup low-calorie French-style
>   salad dressing
> 1 pound calves liver, cut 1/2
>   inch thick

Marinate mushrooms in salad dressing for 30 minutes. Meanwhile, remove membrane from calves liver; cut in serving-sized pieces.

Drain mushrooms, reserving marinade. Brush both sides of liver with reserved marinade. Broil 3 inches from heat for 4 minutes. Turn; top with mushrooms. Broil till liver is tender, about 4 minutes longer. Serves 4.

Pickled Shrimp

A tasty appetizer—

Cover 1 pound fresh or frozen shrimp in shells with boiling water; add 1/4 cup celery leaves, 2 tablespoons mixed pickling spices, 1 1/2 teaspoons salt. Cover; simmer for 5 minutes. Drain; peel and devein shrimp under cold water.

Mix shrimp, 1/2 cup sliced onion, and 4 bay leaves; arrange in shallow dish. Combine 3/4 cup low-calorie Italian salad dressing, 1/3 cup white vinegar, 1 tablespoon capers with liquid, 1 teaspoon celery seed, 1/2 teaspoon salt, and few drops bottled hot pepper sauce; mix well. Pour over shrimp mixture. Cover; marinate in refrigerator at least 24 hours, spooning marinade over shrimp occasionally. Makes about 2 1/2 cups pickled shrimp and onions.

Accent the flavor of fresh or canned fruits with sweet-sour Celery Seed Dressing. Substitute poppy seed for celery seed, and use this delicious dressing on vegetable salads, too.

Herbed Steak Broil

Sure to become an over-the-coals favorite—

½ cup clear French salad dressing
with herbs and spices
½ cup dry sherry
2 tablespoons sliced green onion
1 tablespoon Worcestershire sauce
Dash pepper
1 2½- to 3 pound chuck steak, cut
1½ inches thick

Combine salad dressing, dry sherry, sliced green onion, Worcestershire sauce, and pepper. Pour over steak in shallow dish. Cover and marinate several hours at room temperature or overnight in refrigerator, turning at least once and spooning sauce over occasionally. Drain, reserving marinade. Broil steak over hot coals for 40 to 50 minutes, turning every 10 to 15 minutes, and brush with marinade. Steak will be rare; cook longer for desired doneness. Makes 6 to 8 servings.

Tuna-Berry Sandwiches

A tasty tuna and cranberry combination—

1 6½- or 7-ounce can tuna,
drained and flaked
¼ cup finely chopped celery
2 tablespoons chopped walnuts
¼ cup mayonnaise or salad
dressing
8 slices white bread
1 8-ounce can jellied cranberry
sauce, sliced ¼ inch thick
• • •
2 slightly beaten eggs
3 tablespoons milk
Dash salt

In mixing bowl combine flaked tuna, finely chopped celery, chopped walnuts, and mayonnaise or salad dressing. Spread filling on 4 slices bread. Arrange cranberry slices atop filling; top with remaining bread.

In shallow bowl combine slightly beaten eggs, milk, and the dash salt. Dip sandwiches in egg mixture. Grill on medium-hot, lightly greased griddle till browned, about 6 to 8 minutes, turning once. Makes 4 servings.

SALAD OIL—Any one of several vegetable oils commonly used in making salad dressings. This type of oil is usually extracted from corn, olives, cottonseed, safflower seeds, soybeans, or peanuts.

After extraction, the oil is refined, bleached, and deodorized. Another process frequently used for salad oil is called winterizing. This consists of chilling the oil and then filtering out any crystals. If salad oil does not undergo winterizing, it will become cloudy if stored at refrigerator temperatures.

Besides its use in salad dressings, salad oil is used also in baked goods and for frying foods. In fact, salad oil can be used wherever vegetable oil or cooking oil is called for. (See also *Fat*.)

Rare Roast Beef Salad

1 1-pound T-bone steak, cut
1 inch thick
⅔ cup salad oil
1 teaspoon grated lemon peel
⅓ cup lemon juice
1 teaspoon Worcestershire sauce
1 teaspoon prepared mustard
½ teaspoon salt
• • •
4 ounces natural Swiss cheese,
cut in strips (1 cup)
¼ cup diced green pepper
2 tablespoons sliced green onion
6 cups torn romaine
Dash salt
Dash freshly ground pepper

Trim fat from steak. In screw-top jar combine oil, lemon peel and juice, Worcestershire sauce, mustard, and salt. Cover and shake vigorously to blend. Pour over steak in shallow baking dish. Cover; marinate 4 hours at room temperature or overnight in refrigerator. Drain off marinade; reserve for dressing. Broil steak 3 inches from heat to rare doneness, about 5 minutes per side; cool. Slice steak into thin strips; chill.

In salad bowl arrange steak strips, cheese strips, diced green pepper, and sliced onion over the 6 cups torn romaine. Toss with some of the reserved marinade, dash salt, and freshly ground pepper. Makes 4 servings.

Spiced Applesauce Bread

1¼ cups applesauce
1 cup granulated sugar
½ cup salad oil
2 eggs
3 tablespoons milk
2 cups sifted all-purpose flour
1 teaspoon baking soda
½ teaspoon baking powder
1 teaspoon ground cinnamon
¼ teaspoon *each* salt, ground
  nutmeg, and ground allspice
¾ cup chopped pecans
¼ cup brown sugar

Thoroughly combine first 5 ingredients. Sift together flour, baking soda, baking powder, ½ *teaspoon* cinnamon, salt, nutmeg, and allspice. Stir into applesauce mixture; beat well. Fold in ½ *cup* pecans; turn into well-greased 9x5x3-inch loaf pan. For topping, combine remaining pecans, brown sugar, and remaining cinnamon; sprinkle over batter. Bake at 350° for 1 hour. Remove from pan; cool on rack.

SALAMI *(suh lä′ mē)*—A highly seasoned sausage made of pork and usually beef. Two types of salami are commonly available—hard and soft. Hard salami is an air-dried sausage that will keep without refrigeration until it is cut. Fresh (soft) salami has not been dried and must be kept refrigerated. Differences in seasonings and the proportion of pork to beef account for the various kinds of salami such as Italian, Genoa, and cotto salami.

Use salami on appetizer trays, plates of cold cuts, and in hot dishes, especially Italian dishes. (See also *Sausage*.)

Salami-Cheese Salad

6 cups torn lettuce
1 cup sliced salami, cut in
  quarters
4 ounces natural Swiss cheese,
  cut in strips
½ cup sliced pitted ripe olives
3 tablespoons chopped canned
  pimiento
1 2-ounce can anchovy fillets,
  drained and chopped
⅓ cup salad oil
3 tablespoons wine vinegar
½ clove garlic, crushed

Combine lettuce, salami, cheese, olives, pimiento, and anchovies. In screw-top jar combine oil, vinegar, and garlic for dressing. Cover; shake well. Makes 8 servings.

Aladdin's Salad Bowl

4 cups torn lettuce
2 cups torn endive
1 4-ounce package sliced, jellied
  beef loaf, cut in strips
1 4-ounce package sliced
  salami, cut in strips
6 ounces sliced natural Muenster
  cheese, cut in strips
2 hard-cooked eggs, sliced
½ cup mayonnaise
¼ cup Russian salad dressing

Combine lettuce and endive in salad bowl. Arrange beef, salami, cheese, and egg slices atop greens. Season to taste with salt and pepper. Combine mayonnaise and Russian dressing. Serve with salad. Serves 4 to 6.

At left: Highly seasoned dry salami is great for snacking. Garlic is one of the predominant flavors in this chewy sausage, which is air-dried but not smoked.

At right: Scattered whole peppercorns and a mild garlic flavor distinguish cotto salami. This pork and beef sausage is both cooked and smoked during processing.

SALISBURY STEAK *(sôlz′ ber′ ē, -buh rē)*— A mixture of ground beef formed into a patty. This mixture often contains bread or cracker crumbs, egg, onion, green pepper, and seasonings, and it may be served with a sauce. The patty can be broiled, panbroiled, or panfried. Salisbury steak closely resembles a hamburger patty.

Salisbury Steak

1 beaten egg
½ cup soft bread crumbs
¼ cup finely chopped onion
2 tablespoons finely chopped
  green pepper
1½ teaspoons salt
¼ teaspoon pepper
2 pounds ground beef

Combine egg, crumbs, onion, green pepper, salt, and pepper. Add the ground beef and mix well. Shape into 6 patties, ¾ inch thick. Broil 3 inches from heat for 6 minutes. Turn and broil 4 minutes longer. Makes 6 servings.

SALLY LUNN—A coffee cake-type bread most often leavened with yeast; however, baking powder is sometimes used in place of the yeast. This bread may be baked in a loaf pan, square pan, muffin pan, Turk's head pan, or 10-inch tube pan. It is especially delicious when served hot.

This coffee bread is said to have been named after an eighteenth-century English woman by the name of Sally Lunn. She baked and sold the bread in her tea-shop, which was located in Bath, England.

Sally Lunn

Good for brunch or breakfast—

1 package active dry yeast
¼ cup warm water
¾ cup milk, scalded
3 tablespoons butter or margarine
3 tablespoons sugar
2 eggs
3½ cups sifted all-purpose flour
1¼ teaspoons salt

Soften yeast in warm water (110°). Cool milk to lukewarm. Add to yeast mixture and set aside. Cream butter and sugar. Add eggs, one at a time, beating after each addition. Add flour and salt to creamed mixture *alternately* with yeast mixture, beating well after each addition. Beat till smooth. Cover; let rise in warm place till double, about 1 hour.

Beat down and pour into a well-greased Turk's head mold or a 10-inch tube pan. Let the dough rise till double, about 30 minutes. Bake at 350° till golden brown and crusty, about 40 to 45 minutes. Serve hot.

SALMAGUNDI *(sal′muh gun′ dē)*—1. A medley or mixture of foods usually containing chopped meat (often leftover) or fish, vegetables, and eggs. 2. A salad made of cooked meat served with mayonnaise or salad dressing. The origin of the word salmagundi is not known, although some say it was named after a recipe prepared by an eighteenth-century French chef, Salmis De Gonde. Today, it is associated with a number of mixed casserole dishes.

Salmagundi Bake

1 8-ounce can tomato sauce
¾ cup uncooked long-grain rice
1 cup chopped onion
½ cup chopped green pepper
1 teaspoon salt
  Dash pepper
1 pound ground beef
1 teaspoon salt
1 12-ounce can whole kernel corn,
  drained
1 to 2 teaspoons chili powder
1 8-ounce can tomato sauce

Combine 1 can tomato sauce, uncooked rice, 1 cup water, onion, green pepper, 1 teaspoon salt, and pepper. Turn into a 2-quart casserole. Layer uncooked beef on top. Sprinkle with 1 teaspoon salt. Evenly spread the drained corn over beef. Add chili powder to 1 can tomato sauce; pour mixture over corn.

Cover and bake at 375° for 1 hour. Uncover and bake till rice is tender, about 10 minutes longer. Garnish with crisp bacon curls, if desired. Makes 6 to 8 servings.

SALMI *(sal' mē)*—An elaborate dish of French origin made traditionally with wild game birds such as pheasant. After the bird is partially roasted, the meat is removed from the bones and cooked with truffles and mushrooms in a white wine sauce. The sauce can be prepared in a chafing dish at the table. The mixture is then served on bread spread with pate.

SALMON—A finfish that lives in the Pacific and Atlantic oceans and also in some freshwater lakes. It has an elongated body with a pointed snout. The word salmon comes from the Latin word *saline*, meaning to leap, which is exactly what salmon do as they make their way back to native streams for the spawning season.

From early times, salmon was important as a food to the American Indian, especially the Indians of the Pacific Northwest. Salmon is mentioned often in Indian legend as being symbolic of the whale in the biblical story of Jonah.

Early colonists and pioneers ate fresh salmon, too. In fact, many of these people settled in the New England area because of the abundance of salmon. Both the Indians and the colonists smoked the fish as a method of preserving it for use when the fish were not "in season." Since those early times, the waters along the East Coast have been overfished and polluted; consequently, salmon have become scarce along the Eastern seaboard.

Types of salmon: Because of the scarcity of Atlantic salmon, the majority of these food fish are found in the Pacific Ocean. The largest percent come from the Pacific Northwest—Alaska, Washington, and Oregon.

The following life cycle is true for all types of Pacific salmon. Prior to the spawning season, salmon courageously swim back to their native freshwater streams, often leaping up waterfalls and traveling several hundred miles. As they reach the mouth of the river where they spawn, the salmons' stomachs shrink and their throats narrow, which lessens their appetites. This makes the salmon flesh watery, soft, and light in color. Shortly after spawning, most of the adult Pacific salmon die, and only a small number of the newly hatched fish ever reach maturity. These salmon stay in the fresh water until they are old enough to migrate to the ocean, and then they repeat this cycle.

There are five major types of salmon—chinook, coho, sockeye, pink, and chum. The largest of these types, the chinook, is named after an Indian word meaning spring. It is also called the king salmon, probably because it averages between 20 and 25 pounds. The flesh of this fish is usually very red, but it can be almost white, especially at spawning time. The flesh of chinook salmon is firm.

Another type of salmon, the coho, is also called the silver salmon because of its silvery skin. The flesh of this type fades as it is cooked. Coho salmon average about nine pounds, but they can weigh up to 30 pounds.

One of the most familiar types of salmon to homemakers is the sockeye, also named the blueback or red salmon. The flesh is deep red, firm, sweet, and contains much oil. The sockeye averages between three and five pounds.

The pale-fleshed, pink or humpback salmon is the smallest salmon and weighs three to six pounds. It has a moderate amount of oil and breaks into small flakes.

The last type of Pacific salmon is the chum, keta, or dog salmon. It has the palest flesh with the least amount of oil of all the types. Chum salmon is used for canning and seafood dishes where color and texture are not important.

The salmon in the Atlantic Ocean average in weight from 10 to 20 pounds. Their life cycle is different from the Pacific salmon in that they survive several spawnings. The few salmon that are still taken from the Atlantic come mostly from the east coast of Canada and Maine. Nova Scotia salmon is considered a delicacy. The eastern salmon has a paler flesh.

The color of the different types varies from deep red to pale pink. These types, ranging from the deepest red to the lightest pink, are sockeye, chinook, coho, pink, and chum. The deeper red the color, the higher the oil content, and most often, the higher the price the fish will command.

Nutritional value: Salmon contains some sodium, calcium, phosphorus, iodine, vitamin A, and the B vitamins thiamine and riboflavin. The calcium content is higher if the skin, bones, and liquid are included when preparing canned salmon.

Salmon is a fat fish, and the fat is polyunsaturated, the type recommended for low cholesterol diets. Salmon is also a good source of protein, which is greatly needed for body building.

As far as calories are concerned, one-half cup of canned chinook salmon equals 262 calories; one-half cup canned pink salmon equals 176 calories; and one-half cup canned sockeye equals 213 calories. A 3½-ounce uncooked portion of Atlantic salmon equals 217 calories; of chinook salmon equals 222 calories; and of pink salmon equals 119 calories. A 3½-ounce portion of smoked salmon has 176 calories.

How to select: Salmon comes in a variety of forms—smoked, salted, canned, fresh, and frozen. Whole fresh salmon should have the same general characteristics as any other fresh fish—firm flesh, fresh odor, bright and clear eyes, and shiny skin. Fresh fillets, steaks, and rounds should have a fresh-cut appearance and a fresh odor. Frozen fish have no odor.

Poached Salmon with Cucumber Sauce is a make-ahead main dish. Both salmon and sauce are chilled thoroughly before serving. Remember this tasty sauce to dress up canned salmon.

Canned salmon is identified by the name of the species. The grades from high to low are sockeye, chinook, coho, pink, and chum. Choose chinook and sockeye for salads, as they are deep in color and break into large flakes. Coho is also good for salads and creamed dishes. Pink and chum salmon break into small flakes and are tasty in salmon loaves, sandwiches, soups, and casseroles.

How to store: Keep frozen salmon solidly frozen and tightly wrapped in freezer until ready to use. It should be used within six months. Store fresh salmon in the refrigerator and use within a day or two after purchase. Store canned salmon on the shelf in a cool, dry place.

How to use: Since salmon is a fat fish, it can be prepared by any of the basic fish cooking methods—baking, broiling, frying, poaching, and steaming.

Fresh or frozen salmon lends itself to many elegant dishes. Poached salmon, for example, is excellent with a sauce.

Salmon with Cucumber Sauce

        1 quart water
    1½ tablespoons salt
        2 tablespoons lemon juice
        6 fresh or frozen salmon steaks*
        1 unpeeled cucumber
    ½ cup dairy sour cream
    ¼ cup mayonnaise
        1 tablespoon minced parsley
        2 teaspoons grated onion
        2 teaspoons vinegar
    ¼ teaspoon salt
        Dash pepper
        Shredded lettuce

In large skillet bring water, 1½ tablespoons salt, and lemon juice to boiling. Add 3 salmon steaks. Simmer till fish flakes, 5 to 10 minutes. Remove steaks with slotted spatula. Repeat with remaining salmon in same cooking water. Chill salmon thoroughly.

Meanwhile, prepare cucumber sauce by shredding enough cucumber to make 1 cup (do not drain). Add remaining ingredients, except salmon and lettuce. Blend well. Chill.

Arrange salmon on a bed of shredded lettuce. Serve with lemon wedges, if desired, and cucumber sauce. Makes 6 servings.

*If using frozen salmon, thaw before cooking.

Salmon with Crab Sauce

        2 cups water
        2 lemon slices
    ½ teaspoon salt
    ½ teaspoon dillseed
        1 bay leaf
        2 12-ounce packages frozen salmon
            steaks (6 steaks), partially
            thawed
        1 cup chicken broth
        4 teaspoons cornstarch
    ¼ cup dairy sour cream
        2 tablespoons butter or margarine
            Dash ground nutmeg
        1 7½-ounce can crab meat, drained,
            flaked, and cartilage removed

In a large skillet combine water, lemon slices, salt, dillseed, and bay leaf; heat to boiling. Add salmon steaks and return to boiling. Reduce heat; simmer till salmon flakes easily when tested with a fork, 5 to 10 minutes.

Meanwhile, prepare crab sauce by gradually stirring cold broth into cornstarch in saucepan. Cook quickly, stirring constantly, till mixture is thick and bubbly. Cook 1 minute more. Then, remove from heat. Stir in sour cream, butter or margarine, and nutmeg; add crab meat. Heat through *but do not boil.*

Place salmon on warm serving platter. Serve with crab sauce. Makes 6 servings.

Dilled Salmon Steaks

Place 4 fresh or frozen salmon steaks in lightly greased baking dish (thaw steaks if they are frozen). Combine 2 tablespoons lemon juice and 2 teaspoons instant minced onion; sprinkle over salmon. Season with ½ teaspoon salt and dash pepper. Bake, uncovered, at 400° till fish flakes easily, about 15 to 20 minutes. Remove the fish from the oven.

Spread ¼ cup dairy sour cream over salmon. Sprinkle with 1 teaspoon grated lemon peel and ½ teaspoon dried dillweed. Return to oven; bake 3 minutes longer. Makes 4 servings.

Salmon Steaks

    4 fresh or frozen salmon steaks,
        1 inch thick
    1/3 cup butter, melted
    1 teaspoon Worcestershire sauce
    1 teaspoon grated onion
    1/4 teaspoon paprika

Place steaks in shallow baking pan (thaw frozen steaks). Blend remaining ingredients; brush some lightly on salmon. Sprinkle with salt. Bake at 350° till fish flakes easily, about 25 minutes. Pass remaining sauce. Serves 4.

Grilled Salmon Steaks

    1/2 cup salad oil
    1/4 cup snipped parsley
    1/4 cup lemon juice
    2 tablespoons grated onion
    1/2 teaspoon dry mustard
    1/4 teaspoon salt
        Dash pepper
    6 fresh or frozen salmon steaks

Combine oil, parsley, lemon juice, onion, mustard, salt, and pepper. Mix well. Place salmon steaks in shallow dish (thaw steaks if frozen). Pour on marinade mixture. Let stand at room temperature for 2 hours, turning occasionally. (Or marinate in refrigerator for 4 to 6 hours.) Drain, reserving marinade.

Place fish in greased, wire broiler basket. Broil over *medium-hot* coals till slightly brown, about 8 to 10 minutes. Baste with marinade and turn carefully. Brush again with marinade. Broil till fish flakes easily with a fork, about 8 to 10 minutes longer. Makes 6 servings.

Canned salmon adds variety to the menu because it can be used for many different types of dishes, from salads that are cold to piping-hot casserole dishes.

Fancy enough for a bridge luncheon

← A perky lemon twist and curly endive trim Salmon-Avocado Mold, which is frosted with an avocado-sour cream mixture.

Salmon-Avocado Mold

    1 envelope unflavored gelatin
        (1 tablespoon)
    2 tablespoons sugar
    1 tablespoon lemon juice
    1 tablespoon vinegar
    2 teaspoons grated onion
    1/2 teaspoon prepared horseradish
    1 16-ounce can salmon, drained
        and flaked
    1/2 cup mayonnaise
    1/3 cup sliced pitted ripe olives
    1/4 cup finely chopped celery
    1 large avocado
    1/2 cup dairy sour cream

In saucepan soften gelatin in 1 cup cold water. Stir over low heat till gelatin is completely dissolved. Stir in sugar, lemon juice, vinegar, onion, 1/2 teaspoon salt, and horseradish. Chill till the mixture is partially set.

Fold in flaked salmon, mayonnaise, olives, and celery. Spoon into a 3 1/2-cup mold; chill till the gelatin mixture is firm.

To prepare avocado dressing, peel and mash avocado. Blend the mashed avocado (about 2/3 cup), sour cream, and 1/2 teaspoon salt. Chill. Unmold salmon salad onto serving platter. Spread avocado dressing mixture evenly over outside of salad. If desired, garnish with curly endive and lemon twist. Serves 4.

Salmon-Filled Tomatoes

    6 medium tomatoes
    1 16-ounce can salmon, drained and
        broken into small chunks
    1 1/2 cups diced, peeled cucumber
    1/2 cup mayonnaise
    1 tablespoon chopped onion
    1 tablespoon chopped, canned
        pimiento
        Lettuce

Scoop out centers of tomatoes. Invert; chill. Combine salmon, cucumber, mayonnaise, onion, pimiento, 1/4 teaspoon salt, and dash pepper. Chill the salad mixture thoroughly.

Just before serving, sprinkle insides of tomatoes with salt. Spoon chilled salmon mixture into tomato cavities. Serve on lettuce-lined plates. Makes 6 servings.

For something special, serve smoked salmon on black bread or pumpernickel and accompany with cucumber slices and lemon wedges.

Salmon and Potato Chip Casserole

An easy main dish to fix when there are a large number of people to serve—

    ½ cup butter or margarine
    1 large onion, chopped (1 cup)
    ¼ cup all-purpose flour
    5 10½-ounce cans condensed
        cream of mushroom soup
    4 cups milk
        • • •
    1¼ pounds potato chips, coarsely
        crushed (12 cups)
    5 16-ounce cans salmon,
        drained and flaked
    2 10-ounce packages frozen peas,
        cooked and drained

In a 3-quart saucepan melt butter; add onion and cook till tender but not brown. Blend in flour, stirring till bubbly. Stir in soup. Gradually add milk, stirring till smooth. Set aside about *2 cups* crushed potato chips. In two 13x 9x2-inch metal baking pans, layer the remaining potato chips, salmon, peas, and the soup mixture alternately. Sprinkle reserved chips over top. Bake at 350° till heated through, about 40 to 45 minutes. Makes 25 servings.

Salmon Loaf

    1 beaten egg
    ½ cup milk
    2 cups soft bread crumbs
        (about 3 slices)
    1 tablespoon butter, melted
    1 tablespoon chopped onion
    ½ teaspoon salt
    1 16-ounce can salmon,
        drained and flaked
        • • •
    Piquant Sauce

In a bowl combine egg, milk, soft bread crumbs, melted butter, chopped onion, and salt; add salmon; mix thoroughly. Shape into a loaf on a greased shallow baking pan or in a 7½x3¾x 2¼-inch loaf pan. Bake at 350° for 35 to 40 minutes. Serve with Piquant Sauce or creamed peas. Makes 3 or 4 servings.

Piquant Sauce: Cook 2 tablespoons chopped green onion in 3 tablespoons butter or margarine till onion is tender but not brown. Blend in 2 tablespoons all-purpose flour, ½ teaspoon dry mustard, ½ teaspoon salt, and dash pepper. Add 1¼ cups milk and 1 teaspoon Worcestershire sauce. Cook, stirring constantly, till the sauce thickens and bubbles.

Salmon Balls in Caper Sauce

Drain one 16-ounce can salmon, reserving liquid; flake salmon. In a bowl combine 2 beaten eggs, 1 cup soft bread crumbs (about 1½ slices), 2 tablespoons snipped parsley, 1 tablespoon grated onion, ½ teaspoon salt, ½ teaspoon grated lemon peel, 2 teaspoons lemon juice, and dash pepper. Mix ingredients. Shape into 8 balls; place in a medium skillet.

Combine ½ cup dry white wine and reserved salmon liquid. Add water to make 2 cups liquid. Pour over salmon balls. Heat to boiling. Reduce heat; cover and simmer 10 minutes. Remove the salmon balls to serving dish.

Combine 2 tablespoons softened butter or margarine and 2 tablespoons all-purpose flour. Stir into hot liquid. Cook and stir over high heat till the mixture thickens and bubbles. Stir in ½ cup light cream, 1 tablespoon snipped parsley, and 1 tablespoon capers, drained. Heat the mixture to boiling. Serve the sauce over cooked salmon balls. Makes 4 servings.

Salmon Roll-Ups

 1 7¾-ounce can salmon, drained
   and flaked
 1 beaten egg
 1 teaspoon dried parsley flakes
 1 teaspoon instant minced onion
 ½ teaspoon dried dillweed
 1 8-ounce package refrigerated
   crescent rolls (8 rolls)

 • • •

 2 tablespoons butter or margarine
 2 tablespoons all-purpose flour
 ½ teaspoon salt
   Dash pepper
 1 cup milk
 2 ounces sharp process American
   cheese, shredded (½ cup)
 2 beaten egg yolks
 1 tablespoon lemon juice

Combine salmon, egg, parsley, onion, and dill-weed. Separate crescent rolls and spread each with about 1 tablespoon of the salmon mixture. Roll up from wide end. Bake on baking sheet at 375° for 12 to 15 minutes.

Serve with Cheese Sauce. In saucepan melt butter; blend in flour, salt, and pepper. Add milk; cook and stir until thickened and bubbly. Stir in cheese, egg yolks, and lemon juice; heat till cheese melts. Makes 4 servings.

Salmon Tetrazzini

Cook 4 ounces spaghetti according to package directions; drain. Meanwhile, drain one 16-ounce can salmon, reserving liquid. Add milk to salmon liquid to make 2 cups. Break salmon into large pieces; set aside.

Melt 2 tablespoons butter or margarine in a saucepan. Blend in 2 tablespoons all-purpose flour, ¼ teaspoon salt, dash pepper, and dash ground nutmeg. Add salmon liquid and milk all at once. Cook over medium heat, stirring constantly, till mixture is thickened and bubbly. Add 2 tablespoons dry red wine.

Stir in cooked spaghetti; one 3-ounce can sliced mushrooms, drained; and salmon pieces. Turn into 1-quart casserole. Combine 2 table-spoons fine dry bread crumbs and 2 tablespoons grated Parmesan cheese. Sprinkle cheese-crumb mixture over top. Bake at 350° for 35 to 40 minutes. Makes 6 servings.

Salmon Casserole

Cook ¼ cup chopped onion and ¼ cup chopped celery in 1 tablespoon butter till tender. Blend cooked vegetables with one 7¾-ounce can salmon, flaked (with liquid); one 10½-ounce can condensed cream of mushroom soup; ½ cup shredded sharp process American cheese; and 2 cups cooked rice. Turn the mixture into a 1-quart casserole. Sprinkle ½ cup buttered soft bread crumbs atop. Bake at 350° for about 30 minutes. Makes 4 servings.

Smoked salmon is available in slices that make delicious main dishes, appetizers, and sandwiches. Cured and smoked red salmon is sometimes referred to as lox, a Jewish favorite served with bagels and cream cheese. (See also *Fish.*)

SALMONBERRY—A type of wild raspberry, also called cloudberry, that grows in the Pacific Northwest. (See also *Raspberry.*)

SALMONELLA—A family of bacteria that causes food poisoning, especially in eggs, poultry, milk, fish, and other animal products. The organisms can be destroyed if heated above 165°. (See also *Food Poisoning.*)

SALMON TROUT—Another name for a steelhead salmon. Although it looks like a salmon, this fish is a large trout. It lives in fresh water. (See also *Trout.*)

SALSA *(säl'suh)*—The Italian and Spanish word for sauce or condiment.

SALSIFY—A root vegetable sometimes called oyster plant or vegetable oyster. The root, the part usually eaten, has a mild, oysterlike flavor and the shape of a carrot. It grows up to 10 inches long and is about 2 inches across at the top. Native to Europe, salsify is more popular there than it is in the United States.

When salsify is prepared, it discolors readily, so keep it in water with some type of acid, such as lemon juice. Serve salsify boiled, mashed, riced, or sauced. It can also be cooked, then marinated and served cold. (See also *Vegetable.*)

SALT—1. The household name for sodium chloride (white, granular substance). **2.** To season a food or to preserve meat and fish with salt.

Undoubtedly one of the most important chemical substances known to man, salt is used in cooking primarily as a seasoning and as a preservative for meat and fish. It is also necessary to the diet.

Salt was especially important for preserving foods prior to the advent of refrigeration. It was used to preserve meats for long periods, such as on sailing voyages. Rich and poor alike kept a salt larder—or ate spoiled meat.

Until modern-day mining techniques were developed, the tiny crystals that you sprinkle liberally on your food were an expensive commodity. In fact, the word salary stems from the Latin *salarium*, the monetary allowance that was given to Roman soldiers to buy salt. Salt's importance can be seen, too, in its use in food terms: salad comes from the Latin *salada*, a dish of salted vegetables; and sauce comes from the Latin *salsus*, a salty seasoning, which, by common usage, became sausage.

It's not too difficult to see that when someone was "not worth his salt," he wasn't regarded too highly by others.

How salt is produced: Originally, salt was an impure product, often mixed with other materials. Now, it is available in various qualities and grades for both table and commercial uses. Salt is made by evaporating a concentrated brine (water with a high concentration of salt), or by mining underground rock salt. It is then cleaned, purified, ground, sieved, and graded before it is put on the market.

Types of salt: There are various forms of cooking salt: regular or iodized table salt, or salt flavored with garlic, celery, onion, hickory, or a mixture of seasonings. You can also buy coarse salt, or Kosher salt, which has large crystals, absorbs moisture slowly, and will not cake easily when introduced to moisture; and the familiar rock salt used for freezing homemade ice cream or for cooking some types of shellfish on the half shell.

Nutritional value: Salt is important to the body, for it regulates the water and nutrients that pass in and out of the body tissues. Salt also helps in the digestion of food. In the stomach, chloride from the salt changes into hydrochloric acid, which is a vital part of the digestive juices. In addition, iodized salt is a major source of iodide in areas where the soil and water content of this nutrient are low. This mineral prevents goiter.

Normally, the food consumed each day provides an adequate supply of salt. Occasionally, however, in cases where there is excessive perspiration due to extreme heat, it may be necessary to take salt tablets to replace the salt lost by the body. However, this is more the exception than a common occurrence.

How to use: The principal uses for table salt or flavored salts in cookery are to add flavor to many foods and to bring out the basic flavor in others. Unless special diet restrictions prohibit the use of salt, add it with discretion. Salting with a heavy hand makes food taste of salt. On the other hand, salting too lightly can cause the food to taste insipid.

Flavored salts add a delightful flavor to a variety of foods. In this recipe, onion salt is added to a jiffy bread.

Crescent Roll-Ups

Unroll one package refrigerated crescent rolls (8 rolls) and separate; spread with ½ cup dairy sour cream and sprinkle with ½ teaspoon onion salt. Cook ½ pound bacon till crisp; drain and crumble. Sprinkle over sour cream. Cut each roll lengthwise into 3 equal wedges. Roll up each wedge, starting at point of wedge. Place on greased baking sheet. Bake at 375° till golden brown, about 12 to 15 minutes. Serve warm as appetizers. Makes 24.

Follow recipe directions carefully when adding salt to foods. For example, salt sprinkled on meat that is broiled or panfried causes juices to flow, making the cooked meat a bit dry. Therefore, season the meat after it is browned.

Not only does salt add flavor, but it has additional functions. In yeast breads it restrains a too-rapid growth of the yeast. Salt is also used to pickle and preserve foods such as hams and cucumbers.

Several other types of salt have cooking functions, too. Coarse salt is often sprinkled on bread sticks. Because the crystals absorb moisture so slowly, they will remain in crystals on the top of the bread stick. Rock salt, a coarser type, is used in the preparation of oysters and clams on the half shell. It helps balance the shells during baking. Rock salt is also necessary in the freezing process for homemade ice cream.

Homemade Strawberry Ice Cream

    2 3¾- or 3⅝-ounce packages
          instant vanilla pudding mix
    4 eggs
    ½ cup sugar
    2 cups whipping cream
    4 10-ounce packages frozen
          strawberries, thawed
    1 teaspoon vanilla
    ½ teaspoon red food coloring
          • • •
       Crushed ice
       Rock salt

Prepare pudding following package directions; chill till set. Beat eggs till light and fluffy. Beat in sugar, cream, and pudding. Stir in strawberries, vanilla, and food coloring.

Pour mixture into freezer can, filling only ⅔ full. Adjust dasher and cover. Fit can into freezer. (If using electric ice cream freezer, follow manufacturer's directions.) Pack ice and salt around can, using 6 parts ice to 1 part rock salt. Turn dasher slowly till ice partially melts and forms a brine. Add more ice and salt, as needed. Turn handle constantly till crank turns hard. Remove ice to below lid of can; remove lid and dasher.

To ripen ice cream, plug opening in lid. Cover can with several thicknesses of waxed paper or foil for tight fit; replace lid. Pack more ice and salt (use 4 parts ice to 1 part salt) around can to fill freezer. Cover freezer with heavy cloth or newspapers. Let ice cream ripen about 4 hours. Makes about 2 quarts.

SALT COD—A cod fish that has been split, salted, and dried. (See also *Cod.*)

SALT FISH—Fish that has been preserved by dry-salting or by being put into a salted brine. Salting fish is a technique that has been used since ancient times to prevent fish from spoiling.

Varieties of fish that are commonly salted include cod, bloaters, and herring. The salt must be removed from the fish before it is cooked. The most common procedure for removing the salt is soaking the fish in water for several hours. The water should be changed several times. Then, the fish can be used in entrees and casseroles. (See also *Fish.*)

SALTIMBOCCA (*säl′ tim bôk′ uh*)—An Italian dish consisting of thin slices of ham and veal rolled up around cheese, then cooked in butter in a skillet.

SALT PORK—A thick, fat portion of pork from the belly of the pig that is cured with dry salt. Salt pork is almost all fat, occasionally streaked with lean.

It is used to flavor baked beans and vegetables. Crisp, fried salt pork is frequently an ingredient in chowders. Occasionally, you will find salt pork baked or panfried for a main dish. (See also *Pork.*)

SALT-RISING BREAD—An old-fashioned raised bread that is made without yeast. A mixture of salt, sugar, milk, and sometimes cornmeal is allowed to stand in a warm place until fermentation begins. This leavens the bread.

SALT STICK—A white or rye roll that is shaped like a thick pencil, generously covered with coarse salt crystals.

SAND DAB—A saltwater flatfish related to the flounder. Sand dabs are usually associated with the Pacific Coast; however, small ones are found on the East Coast.

Sand dabs are commonly available fresh near the source of supply. These lean, delicately flavored fish are cooked by boiling, steaming, or frying. They can be baked or broiled if extra butter or a sauce is added. (See also *Flounder.*)

SANDWICH

How to combine breads and fillings to create unique sandwiches for everyday or party fare.

There's hardly a person alive who is not familiar with a variety of sandwich combinations. To some people the word sandwich brings fond memories of peanut butter and jelly spread on bread, while to others it conjures up the thought of mustard-slathered ham and cheese on rye or a flavorful tuna salad sandwich with a crisp piece of lettuce. But no matter how you stack it, a sandwich always has certain basic ingredients—one, two, or more slices of bread (sometimes buttered, sometimes unbuttered) or rolls or buns, plus a filling or well-seasoned spread. As a matter of fact, a sandwich can be almost any food served on or between slices of bread or on or in rolls.

A sandwich can be a meal-in-one such as the heroes, poor boys, or grinders, or a dainty tea sandwich. It can be hot or cold. It can be a finger food or one that necessitates the use of a knife and fork.

Regardless of the combination, sandwiches are internationally popular. In fact, they have become a part of everyday cooking because of their convenience, the food value they contribute to the diet, and because they are an outlet for the creativity of the modern-day homemaker.

Because of the countless variations of sandwiches that are made, it is rather difficult to trace the history of sandwiches. It is said that people of ancient times used their unleavened bread as a wrapper or liner for other foods, similar to today's open-faced sandwich.

He-man sandwich

← Start with a loaf of unsliced bread to make Dilly Beef Cartwheel (see *Beef* for recipe). Then, slice sandwich into separate wedges.

Some authorities say that during pre-Christian times an unleavened wafer spread with honey was eaten by the high priests, and that Rabbi Hillel, the Jewish teacher, invented the custom of eating a sandwich of matzoh spread with bitter herbs. However, the most familiar story credits an Englishman, John Montague, the Fourth Earl of Sandwich, with the invention of the sandwich. It is said that he liked to gamble, and that one day he decided that he would eat while at the gaming tables. He needed a food that could be held in one hand while he continued playing with the other hand. His "sandwich" consisted of a piece of meat between two pieces of bread.

Fellow gamblers began following his example, and the sandwich was popularized and named after the Earl. This was in the eighteenth century. Since then, sandwiches have become common fare.

Basic ingredients: The essential ingredients of a sandwich are bread, sometimes butter, margarine, or salad dressing, and a filling. Other ingredients, such as lettuce and tomato, can also be added for flavor and texture.

Don't discount the importance of bread in a sandwich because it makes up about two-thirds of most sandwiches. Use fresh bread for sandwiches and don't forget to vary the bread you use. Granted, the most popular is the old standby, white bread; however, there are countless other types of breads and rolls that make the perfect base for the sandwiches you prepare. Choose from whole wheat, cracked wheat, light or dark rye, pumpernickel, sourdough, poppy seed, oatmeal, cheese, onion, nut breads, and fruit loaves. For variety, use hamburger or frankfurter buns, English muffins, French or Italian rolls or bread, and the other types of buns, rolls, and biscuits on the bakery shelf.

If possible, leave the crusts on sliced bread to prevent the sandwich from drying out. Exceptions to this are some of the fancy tea and party sandwiches from which crusts are trimmed off for appearance purposes. When using toasted bread for sandwiches, make sure it's fresh and warm. Toast seems to toughen as it cools.

The next ingredient is butter or margarine. Have the butter softened before you begin making sandwiches. Use a flexible spatula or blunt knife for spreading to avoid tearing the bread. Spread the butter to the edges of the slices. Hit a happy medium between too thin and too heavy a spreading. The butter will keep soft fillings from soaking in, yet avoid any dry bites. For a variation, add flavoring to the butter, such as mustard, garlic, or horseradish. In place of the butter, some people prefer to use mayonnaise or salad dressing. The choice is yours.

Now, you're ready for the filling. You'll find that the combinations for sandwich fillings are almost limitless. This is where the homemaker can let her imagination run loose to create a masterpiece.

There are a few points about fillings to keep in mind, however. Keep juicy fillings, jellies, and the like for sandwiches that are going to be eaten before the bread has a chance to become soggy. Also, when choosing meat for the filling, slice the meat paper-thin and stack four or five slices deep. The sandwich will be easier to bite through than if one thick slice is used. Season salad-type mixtures to taste and add salad dressing or mayonnaise to achieve desired consistency. Fillings should be moist, but should not squeeze out between the bread slices.

In addition to homemade fillings, there are many prepared fillings and spreads on the market. Meat spreads and cream cheese spreads are examples of these.

There are also a variety of additional ingredients available to make sandwiches more appealing. A leaf or two of lettuce adds a bit of crispness to a sandwich, while a slice of tomato adds both a flavor note and a touch of color. A slice of pickle also can be added to a sandwich both for its flavor and for its crisp texture. Add these types of ingredients just before eating the sandwich to keep them crisp and fresh and to prevent the bread from becoming soggy. For lunch boxes or picnics, carry these ingredients separately and add at the last minute.

Nutritional value: Because of its component parts, a sandwich is a very nutritious food. Enriched breads contribute B vitamins and iron to the diet. Bread also contains small amounts of calcium and protein. One slice of enriched white bread contains about 62 calories.

Butter, in addition to contributing calories, adds needed fat to the diet. One tablespoon furnishes 100 calories.

Fillings can also add important nutrients to the diet. Meat, poultry, egg, cheese, and peanut butter fillings contribute protein, vitamins, and minerals.

Preparation: To make batches of sandwiches in a hurry, set up an assembly line for easy preparation. Have the fillings ready before you begin and have the butter softened, ready to spread. Line up slices of bread in pairs, side by side, on a cutting surface. Spread all the bread slices with butter out to the edges. Then top alternate slices of bread with the filling. Make all of one type of sandwich at one time, cut (see suggestions in box on page 1972), and wrap individually, sealing well to keep sandwiches fresh.

Storing and freezing: If circumstances prevent you from preparing sandwiches just before they are eaten, you can make them up ahead of time, wrap them well, and refrigerate or freeze till they are needed. When refrigerating sandwiches, wrap in waxed paper, then cover with a dampened towel to keep them moist.

A meal in a sandwich

Deviled ham, cheese, and tomato go into the →
makings for easy Triple-Layered Sandwiches. Add an apple or orange for dessert.

When time permits, make a batch of sandwiches at one time and store them in the freezer. This way you can make good use of leftover meat and poultry that you may have on hand. Spread fresh bread with butter or margarine rather than mayonnaise or salad dressings, since these products tend to separate when frozen. Wrap and tightly seal each sandwich in a moisture-vaporproof material such as clear plastic wrap, foil, or small plastic bags suited for sandwiches. Label with contents and date, then freeze. You can freeze sandwiches up to two weeks.

Take wrapped sandwiches from the freezer in the morning when it's time to tote them, and they'll be thawed and right for eating at lunchtime. Eat them immediately after they are unwrapped because the bread dries out quickly after it has been frozen and thawed.

Sandwiches that freeze best include hard-cooked egg yolk, sliced or ground meat and poultry, tuna or salmon, and peanut butter. Those fillings not recommended for freezing include cheeses (except blue cheese), lettuce, celery, tomatoes, cucumbers, parsley, watercress, white of hard-cooked eggs, and jelly. Avoid very moist fillings that are made with mayonnaise or salad dressing.

Ways to cut a sandwich

● Since smaller sandwich pieces are easier to handle, cut sandwiches into halves, quarters, or thirds. Use a sharp or serrated, long-bladed knife for quick and easy cutting. Stack two or three and cut all at once.

● Cut sandwich crosswise and lengthwise, making four quarters. Or make four triangles by cutting diagonally.

● Cut diagonally forming two triangles.

● Cut sandwich in thirds, either crosswise, diagonally, or into pie-shaped pieces. Or slice the sandwich in half, either lengthwise or diagonally, and cut one of the halves in half, making three smaller sandwiches.

Types of sandwiches

Sandwiches come in cold or hot versions. Some, such as the open-faced sandwiches of Denmark, a three-decker club sandwich, or a hero sandwich by any of its names, are large enough to be the entire main course. Main dish hot sandwiches include hot, sliced meat in gravy, a scrambled egg sandwich called a Denver or Western, and poultry in cream sauce spooned over a slice of toast. Then, there are the dainty, chilled sandwiches for a tea party or an appetizer buffet.

Cold sandwiches: The open-faced sandwich is good to fix when counting calories. By eliminating the extra slice of bread, you trim some calories. But, when piled high with ingredients, it can satisfy the heartiest appetites.

Fruit Wheels

    2 bagels, split and toasted
    1 tablespoon cream cheese
      Ground cinnamon
      Thin peach slices
      Thin honeydew melon slices
      Thin banana slices

Spread bagel halves thinly with cream cheese; sprinkle with ground cinnamon. Arrange fruit slices atop each. Makes 4 sandwiches.

Garden Cottage Cheese Sandwiches

 1½ cups small curd cream-style
       cottage cheese
  ½ cup diced celery
  ¼ cup shredded carrot
  ¼ cup chopped radish
  ½ teaspoon caraway seed
    6 slices thinly sliced white
       bread
      Butter or margarine, softened
      Lettuce

Mash cottage cheese with fork; stir in vegetables and caraway. Chill. Butter bread; top with lettuce. Spread about ⅓ cup cottage cheese mixture atop lettuce. Serves 6.

Tuna Open-Facer

A sandwich especially suited for dieters—

- 1 6½-ounce can dietetic-pack tuna, drained
- ½ cup coarsely grated cabbage
- ¼ cup coarsely grated carrot
- 1 tablespoon sliced green onion
- ⅓ cup low-calorie mayonnaise-type dressing
- 1 tablespoon catsup
- 1 tablespoon lemon juice
- ½ teaspoon seasoned salt
  Dash pepper
- 4 lettuce leaves
- 2 hamburger buns, split and toasted

Break tuna in chunks; combine with cabbage, carrot, and onion. Blend together low-calorie mayonnaise, catsup, lemon juice, seasoned salt, and pepper; add to tuna mixture and toss lightly. Place 1 lettuce leaf on each toasted bun half; spoon tuna salad mixture on top of the lettuce leaves. Makes 4 servings.

Open-Face Sandwich Supreme

Hearty sandwich for a big appetite—

- ½ cup mayonnaise or salad dressing
- ½ cup catsup
- ¼ cup pickle relish
- 2 tablespoons prepared mustard
- 1 tablespoon milk
- 4 slices rye bread
  Butter or margarine, softened
  Leaf lettuce
- 4 ounces brick or provolone cheese (4 slices)
- 8 thin slices cooked roast beef
  Tomato slices
- 2 hard-cooked eggs, sliced
  Bacon curls

Combine mayonnaise, catsup, pickle relish, mustard, and milk. Spread bread with butter. Top with lettuce, cheese, roast beef, and tomato slices. Spoon ¼ cup of the mayonnaise mixture over each; garnish with egg slices and bacon curls. Pass additional dressing. Serves 4.

┌─────────────────────────────┐

❦MENU❦

LOW-CALORIE LUNCHEON
Fresh Fruit Cup
Tuna Open-Facer
Baked Custard
Coffee   Skim Milk

└─────────────────────────────┘

Cold sandwiches with two or more slices of bread make filling lunchtime entrées. And unsliced loaves of French bread an impressive luncheon main dish.

Triple-Layered Sandwiches

- 1 4½-ounce can deviled ham
- 2 tablespoons pickle relish
- 2 tablespoons finely chopped green pepper
- 12 slices whole wheat bread
  Mayonnaise or salad dressing
- 8 tomato slices
- 4 slices mozzarella cheese

Combine first 3 ingredients. Lightly spread 4 slices bread with mayonnaise; spread each with ham. Top each with another slice bread; spread lightly with mayonnaise. Add tomato and cheese. Dot with mayonnaise; top with remaining bread. Halve; secure with wooden picks. Makes 4.

Fish Salad Club Sandwich

Cook one 16-ounce package frozen perch; flake cooked fish (2 cups). Combine perch with ½ cup chopped celery, ½ cup bottled tartar sauce, and ¼ teaspoon salt. Chill. Spread 18 slices toasted bread with softened butter.

Spread about ⅓ cup perch mixture on each of 6 slices toast. Top each with second slice of toast; place lettuce and tomato slices atop. Cover with third slice of toast. Secure with wooden picks and cut sandwich diagonally into quarters. Makes 6 sandwiches.

Quick Cold Sandwich Ideas

Add avocado slices to bacon, lettuce, and tomato sandwiches. Serve open-face with Thousand Island dressing; homemade or bottled.

Add coleslaw with a little prepared mustard to corned beef on rye sandwiches.

Blend softened cream cheese with orange marmalade, cranberry jelly, or crushed pineapple. Spread the mixture on nut bread.

Combine 1 cup chopped cooked chicken or turkey, 1/3 cup well-drained crushed pineapple, 1/3 cup mayonnaise or salad dressing, 2 tablespoons chopped walnuts, and dash salt.

Blend softened cream cheese with chopped pimiento-stuffed green olives or finely chopped candied ginger. Also a good celery stuffer.

Spread some peanut butter on buttered bread slices. Add crumbled cooked bacon, jelly, pickle slices, or thin slices of banana.

Arrange thinly sliced onion or pickle on buttered bread. Spoon a mixture of baked beans and chili sauce atop the onion or pickle.

Arrange thinly sliced radishes on buttered whole wheat or rye bread.

Mix flaked tuna, crab, or lobster with finely chopped celery and blend with mayonnaise.

Moisten sardines and chopped hard-cooked egg with a little lemon juice.

Layer liverwurst, lettuce, and sliced tomato on buttered whole wheat or white bread.

Chop hard-cooked eggs and pimiento-stuffed green olives. Add mayonnaise to moisten. Spread on rye bread and add a leaf of lettuce.

Mix diced cooked chicken, chopped celery, and chopped sweet pickle with mayonnaise.

Mix cottage cheese, finely chopped onion and green pepper, salt, and paprika.

Spread Russian rye bread with mustard sauce. Top with liver sausage and Swiss cheese.

Golden Gate Salad Loaf

    1 unsliced loaf French bread
      Butter or margarine, softened
    1 ½-pound piece bologna, cut in
      ½-inch cubes (2 cups)
  ½ cup sliced radishes
  1/3 cup mayonnaise
  ¼ cup pickle relish
      Dash pepper
    2 cups shredded lettuce

Cut French bread in half lengthwise; wrap top half and store for later use. Cut thin slice off bottom of remaining half to make it sit flat. Scoop out center to make slight hollow; spread inside with softened butter.

Combine bologna and radishes. Blend together mayonnaise, relish, and pepper. Add to bologna mixture; toss lightly. Place shredded lettuce in bottom of hollow; spoon bologna mixture over. Garnish with radishes and sweet pickle slices, if desired. Makes 6 servings.

Shrimp Boat

    3 cups cooked, cleaned shrimp
    1 cup diced celery
    4 hard-cooked eggs, chopped
  1/3 cup sliced green onion
  ¼ cup chopped dill pickle
    2 tablespoons drained capers
      (optional)
    1 cup mayonnaise
    2 tablespoons chili sauce
    2 teaspoons prepared horseradish
    1 teaspoon salt
    1 loaf Vienna bread (11x5 inches)
      Butter or margarine, melted
      Lettuce

Reserve a few large shrimp for garnish; cut up remainder. Combine first 6 ingredients. Blend mayonnaise and next 3 ingredients. Add to shrimp mixture and toss lightly. Chill.

Meanwhile, cut a large, deep wedge out of Vienna loaf to make "boat." Brush the cut surfaces with melted butter. Place loaf on *ungreased* baking sheet. Toast at 350° till lightly browned, 15 minutes. Cool before filling.

Line bread with lettuce; mound with shrimp salad. Trim with whole shrimp. If desired, pass lemon wedges. Cut in 6 to 8 slices.

Hot sandwiches: Perhaps the hamburger or frankfurter (coney) sandwich is at the top of your favorite hot sandwich list. With the addition of a few ingredients, a hamburger is turned into gourmet fare. Grilled sandwiches and the king-sized sandwiches served on a loaf of French bread are also treats for large appetites.

Tangy Kraut Burger

1½ pounds ground beef
  1 8-ounce can sauerkraut,
     drained and snipped
  ¼ cup Italian salad dressing
  1 tablespoon instant minced onion
  ½ teaspoon caraway seed
  ¼ teaspoon salt
  6 hamburger buns, split and
     toasted

Combine ground beef, sauerkraut, dressing, onion, caraway, and salt. Shape into 6 patties, ¾ inch thick. Broil 3 inches from heat for 6 minutes. Turn; broil 6 to 8 minutes longer. Serve in buns. (Top burgers with hot sauerkraut, if desired.) Makes 6 sandwiches.

Quick Hot Sandwich Ideas

Spread French bread slices with butter or margarine and prepared mustard. Spoon on baked beans and top with shredded sharp process American cheese. Broil till cheese melts.

Spread 2 tablespoons seasoned ground beef on sliced bread. Broil about 3 minutes.

Scramble eggs with finely chopped onion, chopped green pepper, and diced ham. Serve the scrambled eggs on toast.

Before forming hamburger patties, spark ground beef with one or more of the following ingredients: Worcestershire sauce, chopped onion, chopped green pepper, soy sauce and ginger, mustard, catsup, pickle relish, barbecue sauce, or prepared horseradish.

Toast bread on one side. Top untoasted side with cheese and tomato slices. Broil to melt cheese. Top with a cooked bacon slice or two.

Hot Dog Burgers

  1 pound ground beef
  ⅓ cup evaporated milk
  3 frankfurters, halved lengthwise
  3 frankfurter buns, split, toasted,
     and buttered

Combine beef, 1 teaspoon salt, dash pepper, and milk. Shape into 6 flat rectangles the size of buns. Press half of a frank into each burger. Broil 3 inches from heat, 8 to 10 minutes; turn once. Serve in buns. Serves 6.

Besides ground beef, there are other ingredients that make great hot sandwiches. Grilled cheese and oven or broiled seafood sandwiches are always popular. Or how about a breakfast main dish made with corn bread and sausage links?

Breakfast Corn Bread Stacks

Prepare one 10-ounce package corn bread mix following package directions. Cut into 6 servings; keep warm. Cook one 8-ounce package brown-and-serve sausage links following package directions. Split lengthwise; keep warm.

In saucepan combine ¼ cup sugar, 2 tablespoons cornstarch, and ⅛ teaspoon salt; stir in 1½ cups orange juice. Cook and stir till thickened and bubbly. Remove from heat; stir in 2 tablespoons butter and 1 orange, peeled and sectioned. Split corn bread in half lengthwise. Layer bottom halves with sausage and a little orange sauce. Replace tops. Spoon sauce over each serving. Serve warm. Serves 6.

❧ **MENU** ❧

LAZY SATURDAY BREAKFAST
Pineapple-Grapefruit Drink
Breakfast Corn Bread Stacks
Cinnamon-Apple Rings
Coffee   Tea

Stroganoff Sandwich

    1 unsliced loaf French bread
    1 pound ground beef
    ¼ cup chopped green onion
    1 cup dairy sour cream
    1 tablespoon milk
    1 teaspoon Worcestershire sauce
    ¾ teaspoon salt
    ⅛ teaspoon garlic powder
    Butter or margarine, softened

    • • •

    2 tomatoes, sliced
    1 green pepper, cut in rings
    4 ounces sharp process American
        cheese, shredded (1 cup)

Cut loaf in half lengthwise; wrap in foil. Heat at 375° for 10 to 15 minutes. In skillet cook beef with onion till meat is browned; drain off fat. Stir in sour cream, milk, Worcestershire sauce, salt, and garlic powder; heat, *but do not boil.* Butter cut surfaces of bread.

    Spread half of *hot* meat mixture on each loaf half. Arrange tomato slices alternately with green pepper rings atop meat. Sprinkle with cheese. Place on baking sheet; bake at 375° for 5 minutes. Cut each half in 4 slices.

Pizza by the Yard

    1 unsliced loaf French bread
    1 6-ounce can tomato paste
    ⅓ cup grated Parmesan cheese
    ¼ cup finely chopped onion
    ¼ cup chopped, pitted ripe olives
    ¾ teaspoon salt
    ½ teaspoon dried oregano leaves,
        crushed
    ⅛ teaspoon pepper
    1 pound ground beef
    4 tomatoes, sliced (16 slices)
    1 8-ounce package sliced sharp
        process American cheese

Cut loaf in half lengthwise. Combine tomato paste, Parmesan cheese, onion, olives, salt, oregano, and pepper. Add meat; mix well. Spread atop loaf halves. Place on baking sheet. Bake at 400° for 20 minutes. Remove from oven; top with tomato slices. Cut cheese in 1-inch strips. Crisscross strips atop tomatoes. Bake 5 minutes. Makes 4 or 5 servings.

Meat Loaf Splits

For easier eating, split sandwich in center—

    1 unsliced loaf Italian or French
        bread
    ¼ cup butter, softened
    ⅛ teaspoon garlic powder
    8 slices process American cheese
    4 slices leftover meat loaf, sliced
        ⅜ inch thick
    Grated Parmesan cheese

Cut ends from loaf; store for later use. Slice loaf crosswise into 8 pieces. In each piece make 3 slashes, *almost to bottom.*

    Blend butter with garlic powder; spread on all cut surfaces of bread. Quarter cheese and meat slices. Place meat slice between 2 cheese slices; repeat to make 16 meat-cheese stacks.

    Insert stacks in the *two* end slashes in each bread piece. Sprinkle sides of sandwiches with grated Parmesan cheese. Place on baking sheet. Bake at 400° till lightly browned, 8 to 10 minutes. Makes 8 servings.

Corned Beef Hash Burgers

    1 15-ounce can corned beef hash
    ⅓ cup dairy sour cream
    1 tablespoon pickle relish
    1 teaspoon prepared horseradish

    • • •

    8 onion rolls, split and toasted
    8 slices tomato
    8 ounces process American
        cheese (8 slices)

Combine corned beef hash, sour cream, pickle relish, and horseradish; spread about ¼ cup mixture on bottom halves of rolls. Broil 3 to 4 inches from heat till hot, about 5 minutes. Top each with a tomato slice, then a cheese slice; broil just till cheese melts. Cover with tops of rolls. Makes 8 sandwiches.

Teen-age party favorites

Vary sandwiches with French bread loaves → by preparing Stroganoff Sandwich and Meat Loaf Splits, both hot from the oven.

❧MENU❧

AFTER THE GAME

Mexi-Taco Sandwiches

Pickles   Olives

Raisin-Sugar Cookies

Hot Chocolate

Mexi-Taco Sandwiches

      1 pound ground beef
    ½ cup chopped onion

            • • •

      1 8-ounce can tomato sauce
      1 teaspoon Worcestershire sauce
    ¼ teaspoon chili powder
    ⅛ teaspoon garlic powder
   1½ cups corn chips, crushed (½ cup)
    12 hamburger buns, split and
         toasted
      3 cups shredded lettuce
      2 tomatoes, diced
      3 ounces natural Cheddar cheese,
         shredded (¾ cup)
         Taco sauce

Cook beef and onion till meat is browned and onion is tender. Add tomato sauce, next 3 ingredients, add ¼ teaspoon salt. Mix well; simmer 10 minutes. Fold in corn chips. Immediately spoon mixture onto toasted bun halves. Top with lettuce, tomato, cheese, and tops of buns. Pass taco sauce. Makes 12 servings.

Paul Revere Cheesewiches

Using 1 package refrigerated biscuits (10 biscuits), roll each to a 4-inch circle on a lightly floured surface. Combine 3 ounces natural Cheddar cheese, shredded (¾ cup); 4 slices bacon, crisp-cooked, drained, and crumbled; and 2 tablespoons pickle relish.

   Place a rounded tablespoon of mixture in center of each circle. Fold up 3 sides; pinch edges to seal. Place biscuits on lightly greased baking sheet. Bake at 425° till golden brown, 8 to 10 minutes. Serve warm. Serves 10.

Creole Sandwiches

      2 tablespoons chopped onion
      2 tablespoons chopped green
         pepper
      1 tablespoon butter or margarine
      1 8-ounce can whole tomatoes,
         cut up
      3 tablespoons sliced, pimiento-
         stuffed green olives
      1 teaspoon sugar
    ¼ teaspoon salt
         Dash garlic salt
         Dash pepper
      4 frozen fish portions
      4 hamburger buns, split and
         toasted

In small saucepan cook onion and green pepper in butter or margarine till tender but not brown. Stir in tomatoes, olives, sugar, salt, garlic salt, and pepper. Simmer till thickened, about 15 to 20 minutes. Panfry fish portions according to package directions. Butter buns, if desired. Place fish portions on bottom halves of buns. Spoon some sauce over fish. Then, put tops of buns in place. Makes 4.

Salmon-Blue Cheese Broilers

      1 16-ounce can salmon, drained
         and flaked
    ⅓ cup mayonnaise
      1 3-ounce can chopped mushrooms,
         drained
      2 tablespoons crumbled blue
         cheese
      8 slices white bread, toasted
         and buttered
         Grated Parmesan cheese

Combine salmon with next 3 ingredients. Spread toasted bread with mixture. Sprinkle Parmesan over sandwiches. Broil 5 inches from heat till hot, about 6 to 7 minutes. Serves 8.

Simple-to-fix fishwiches

Tomato mixture adds a colorful and flavorful → touch to Creole Sandwiches. Make plenty of these sandwiches for second helpings.

Party sandwiches: Small, fancy sandwiches arranged on a silver tray or a cheese-frosted sandwich loaf make an impressive showing at an afternoon tea, bridal or baby shower, or cocktail party. The small sandwiches include checkerboards, cornucopias, ribbons, and various-shaped pieces of bread spread with an enticing filling. Many of these tidbits are easy to make, and preparation speeds along once you've mastered the techniques. (See box below for some clues that will be helpful.)

Sandwich loaves are a good choice when you've got a group to feed. The sandwich loaf is more filling than the tiny sandwiches, and it can be used for a luncheon main dish. Choose complementary, yet contrasting flavors for the filling—anything that is easy to cut with a fork, since this sandwich is usually eaten with a fork.

Party sandwich tips

● Freeze bread for meat sandwiches. Then, cut and spread while bread is frozen.

● Trim off crusts for fancy sandwiches.

● Use thinly sliced bread or buy an unsliced loaf of bread and thinly cut it lengthwise. There will be less waste when cutting the bread into shapes.

● Use cookie cutters for fancy shapes.

● Vary the type of bread used for an assortment of colors and flavors.

Teatime Sandwiches

Soften two 3-ounce packages cream cheese. Blend in $\frac{1}{3}$ cup mayonnaise and 2 tablespoons crumbled blue cheese. Add $\frac{1}{2}$ cup finely chopped nuts, $\frac{1}{2}$ teaspoon Worcestershire sauce, $\frac{1}{4}$ teaspoon salt, and $\frac{1}{4}$ teaspoon grated onion; mix well. Chill. Using a cookie or biscuit cutter, cut out bread rounds and spread with butter, then cheese mixture. Makes $1\frac{1}{3}$ cups.

Seafood Diamonds

Combine flaked canned tuna, crab meat, or lobster with an equal part of finely chopped celery. Moisten with mayonnaise or salad dressing, adding lemon juice to taste. Spread mixture on diamonds cut out of whole wheat bread slices. Trim tops with pimiento cutouts.

Orange-Date Fold-Ups

　$\frac{1}{2}$ **cup finely snipped dates**
　$\frac{1}{4}$ **cup finely chopped walnuts**
　$\frac{1}{3}$ **cup orange juice**
　8 **slices white bread**
　　Butter or margarine, softened

Combine dates, nuts, and orange juice; let stand about 20 minutes. Trim crusts from bread; spread slices with butter, then date mixture. Bring two opposite corners of each square together at center. Secure with wooden pick; garnish with sprig of watercress, if desired.

Cornucopias

Trim off the crusts from slices of bread. Spread bread with softened pineapple-cheese spread. Roll bread into a cone shape (cornucopias). Secure, if necessary, with wooden picks. Trim with ripe olive pieces cut in the shape of petals. Chill sandwiches, seam side down.

Party sandwiches include Checkerboards, Orange-Date Fold-Ups, Seafood Diamonds, Cornucopias, and Date-Roll Sandwiches.

For making Ribbon Sandwiches and Checkerboards, cut two loaves bread (white and whole wheat) in six ½-inch thick slices.

For Ribbon Sandwiches, stack two long slices whole wheat and two white bread slices, alternating bread. Slice crosswise.

For Checkerboards, make loaves for Ribbon Sandwiches. Cut in six lengthwise slices. Put four slices together, alternating colors.

Date-Roll Sandwiches

> 1 3-ounce package cream cheese, softened
> 1 tablespoon milk
> 1 tablespoon very finely chopped candied ginger
> Canned date-nut roll

Combine cream cheese, milk, and candied ginger. Slice date-nut roll ⅜ inch thick. Spread half the slices with cheese mixture. Top with remaining slices. Cut a crescent from one side of each sandwich using a round cutter. Remaining piece makes a petal-shaped sandwich.

Ribbon Sandwiches

> 1 unsliced loaf white sandwich bread
> 1 unsliced loaf whole wheat sandwich bread
> 1 5-ounce jar sharp process cheese spread
> ½ cup butter, softened

Remove crusts from bread loaves. Cut each loaf into 6 lengthwise slices ½ inch thick. Beat together cheese and butter. Spread on one side of all but 3 of the white bread slices. Make 3 ribbon loaves by stacking 4 long slices together for each, starting with whole wheat, then alternating types of bread, ending with a slice of white bread not spread with the cheese mixture. Wrap; chill. Thinly slice crosswise.

Checkerboards: Prepare 2 ribbon loaves as for Ribbon Sandwiches. Cut each ribbon loaf into 6 lengthwise slices. Put 4 slices together with cheese mixture, alternating colors of bread, making 3 checkerboard loaves. Wrap and chill. Thinly slice the loaves crosswise.

Diploma Sandwiches

Trim crusts from unsliced sandwich loaf. Slice crosswise in very thin slices. Place slices between dampened towels to keep soft. Add a little pickle relish to canned deviled ham. Spread mixture on bread, rolling up immediately. Place seam side down; cover and chill. Before serving, tie in center with ribbon.

Uses in menus

Appetizer or snack-type sandwiches are a simple answer to the question of what to serve at an afternoon or evening gathering when you don't want to present an entire meal. Accompany the sandwiches with a beverage and perhaps a few relishes or delectable tidbits.

Fruit Tea Sandwiches

> 1 3-ounce package cream cheese, softened
> 2 tablespoons drained, crushed pineapple
> ½ teaspoon grated lemon peel
> ½ cup halved seedless green grapes
> ¼ cup miniature marshmallows
> Raisin or nut bread, buttered

Beat first 3 ingredients and dash salt together till fluffy. Add grapes and marshmallows. Spread between slices of bread. Makes 1 cup.

Party Sandwiches

Soften one 3-ounce package cream cheese; blend in 1 tablespoon milk, 1 teaspoon Worcestershire sauce, and 4 or 5 slices crisp-cooked bacon, crumbled. Cut 2-inch rounds with cookie cutters from white, whole wheat, and rye sliced sandwich loaves. Spread *half* of the rounds (use a variety of breads) with mixture. Top with remaining rounds. If desired, use small hors d'oeuvre cutters to cut shapes from centers of rounds.

❖MENU❖

FOR THE NEW NEIGHBOR
Fruit Tea Sandwiches
Party Sandwiches
Nuts   Mints
Tea   Punch

❖MENU❖

STAG PARTY
Big Western Bean Burgers
Corn Chips
Radishes   Dill Pickles
Spice Cake
Coffee

Often, sandwiches are featured as the main dish for a luncheon, stag supper, picnic, or lunch box. For the ladies, serve a cheese-frosted sandwich loaf. Serve the men a he-man sandwich stacked with meat and cheese or a hearty, hot sandwich on a hamburger bun.

Big Western Bean Burgers

> 2 tablespoons onion soup mix
> 1 18-ounce jar baked beans in molasses sauce
> 1 4-ounce package smoked sliced beef, snipped
> 3 tablespoons frankfurter relish
> 8 sesame seed hamburger buns, split and toasted

In saucepan combine ½ cup water and soup mix; let stand till softened, about 5 minutes. Stir in beans, beef, and relish. Cook over medium heat till heated, stirring occasionally. Spoon onto toasted buns. Makes 8 servings.

Salad Sandwich Tower

For each serving, butter a large, round slice of rye bread. Place, buttered side up, on plate. Add lettuce, then slices of Swiss cheese and slices of chicken or turkey.

Stir ½ cup chili sauce into 1 cup mayonnaise or salad dressing. Pour desired amount of mixture over the sandwich. Top with tomato slice, hard-cooked egg slice, hot cooked bacon, ripe olive slices, and a sprig or two of parsley.

Frosted Ribbon Loaf

- 1 unsliced sandwich loaf
  Butter or margarine, softened
- 1 cup Ham Salad Filling
- 1 cup Egg Salad Filling
- 4 3-ounce packages cream cheese, softened
- ⅓ cup milk
  Snipped parsley

Slice bread lengthwise in 3 layers; trim crusts. Butter layers with the softened butter. Spread first layer with Ham Salad Filling and spread Egg Salad Filling on second layer. Assemble loaf using 2 spatulas to support layers, placing third bread layer on top. Wrap loaf tightly in foil; chill the loaf thoroughly.

Before serving, beat cream cheese with milk till fluffy. Frost top and sides of loaf. Sprinkle with snipped parsley. (Or frost early, cover loosely, and chill.) Makes 10 slices.

Ham Salad Filling: In mixing bowl combine 1 cup ground fully cooked ham, ⅓ cup finely chopped celery, 2 tablespoons drained pickle relish, ½ teaspoon prepared horseradish, and ¼ cup mayonnaise. Makes 1½ cups.

Egg Salad Filling: In mixing bowl combine 4 hard-cooked eggs, chopped; ⅓ cup chopped pimiento-stuffed green olives; 2 tablespoons finely chopped green onion; 2 teaspoons mustard; and ¼ cup mayonnaise. Makes 1½ cups.

The next time you hostess a shower, prepare a Frosted Ribbon Loaf. Most of the work is done ahead of time. Then, at serving time, all you need to do is add a few simple garnishes.

SANGRIA *(sang grē′ uh)*—A refreshing, sweet beverage usually made with wine, fruit, and nutmeg. Ale, beer, and other liquors are sometimes used in place of the wine. The punchlike mixture is poured into tall glasses of crushed ice.

Sangria, which in Spanish means "the act of bleeding," gets its name from the traditional blood red color of the drink, which is obtained by using red wine.

Summer Sangria

    ¾ cup light corn syrup
    ⅓ cup lemon juice
    8 drops yellow food coloring
        • • •
    2 cups sparkling water, chilled
      Ice
    2 cups port

Blend light corn syrup, lemon juice, and yellow food coloring; stir in sparkling water. Divide mixture among 4 tall glasses. Add ice cubes or crushed ice. Then, carefully pour ½ cup of the wine down side of each glass. Serve with straws, if desired. Makes 4 servings.

SANTA CLAUS MELON—A name for the large, oblong, green and gold Christmas melon. (See also *Christmas Melon*.)

SAPODILLA *(sap′ uh dil′ uh)*—A tropical evergreen tree that bears fruit called sapodilla plums. The fruit looks like a russet apple and has large black seeds, orange pulp, soft flesh, and a thin skin. The flavor of this fruit resembles that of a pear, being sweet when ripe.

Sapsago cheese; for appetizers or main dishes.

This tree grows wild in Central America and in northern parts of South America. It is also found in parts of Florida. The sapodilla tree attains a height of about 20 feet. In addition to the fruit that it produces, the tree also yields chicle, which is combined with sugar, caramel, and flavorings in chewing gum.

SAPSAGO CHEESE *(sap′ suh gō′)*—A hard, light green-colored cheese that originated in Glarus, Switzerland. The cheese gets its color and pungent flavor from the four-leaf clovers that are added to the cheese, a tradition that was started by Irish monks who lived in Switzerland.

Sapsago is made with sour skim milk, buttermilk, and sour whey. The curd that forms is cured under light pressure. The mixture then is formed into the shape of a cone about four inches tall and weighing between 1 and 2¼ pounds.

Sapsago is used mostly for grating. The grated cheese is sprinkled over scrambled eggs or salads, or is used in sauces. Purchase the whole or grated cheese at specialty food stores. (See also *Cheese*.)

SARATOGA CHIP—A name for potato chips that originated in Saratoga, New York.

SARDINE *(sär dēn′)*—Various types of fish caught while they are small or immature. The sardine can be a herring, alewife, or pilchard. Herring sardines are taken along the northern Atlantic coast, primarily from Maine. Those from Norway are called brisling or sprat. Pilchards are caught in the Mediterranean Sea, English Channel, and along the Pacific coast.

Sardines, named for the island of Sardinia, have green or blue coloring with a silvery cast. Their habit of rising to the surface at night to feed stirs up organisms that give off a phosphorescent glow. This alerts the fisherman of their position so that nets can be set to capture them. This, however, is only one of the methods that is used to catch the fish. Sardines usually measure three to eight inches and weigh about two ounces.

Processing begins as quickly as the sardines are caught. While they are being pumped aboard, the scales are removed and then the fish are salted. At the cannery, the sardines are washed and precooked, and their heads and tails are removed. Then, they are packed into cans with an oil or sauce, sealed, cooked, and sterilized under inspection.

Not all sardines are canned in this manner. Some are sold fresh, salted and preserved in brine, or smoked. However, the majority on the market are canned with an oil or sauce, such as tomato or mustard.

Fresh sardines are available in April and May. They can be cooked like other fat fish. Frying is one of the most popular methods. All forms of sardines are used as appetizers, in hot or cold sandwiches, snacks, and as an ingredient in preparing main-dish casseroles.

The nutritional value of sardines is found in the high-quality protein, minerals, and B vitamins. One and one half large sardines have 160 calories when raw or 197 when canned in tomato sauce. A 3½-ounce serving canned in brine or mustard sauce has 196 calories. (See *Fish, Herring* for additional information.)

Sardine Appetizer Spread

Trim this unusual spread with a small sprig of parsley or watercress—

>   1 3¾-ounce can sardines in oil, drained
>   ¼ cup butter or margarine, softened
>   2 tablespoons finely chopped green onion
>   2 tablespoons chili sauce
>   1 tablespoon lemon juice
>   ¼ teaspoon dry mustard
>   Few drops bottled hot pepper sauce
>   • • •
>   Rye wafers

Mash the sardines with a fork. Combine with the ¼ cup butter or margarine, onion, chili sauce, lemon juice, the ¼ teaspoon mustard, and hot pepper sauce. Blend the mixture thoroughly. Chill. Let stand at room temperature a few minutes before serving. Serve the spread with crisp rye wafers. Makes ¼ cup spread.

Sardine Sandwiches

>   2 3¾-ounce cans sardines in oil
>   2 hard-cooked eggs, chopped
>   2 tablespoons snipped chives
>   2 tablespoons mayonnaise
>   1 tablespoon lemon juice
>   12 slices whole wheat bread
>   Mayonnaise

Drain sardines and mash. Combine sardines, eggs, chives, 2 tablespoons mayonnaise, and lemon juice. Spread whole wheat bread with additional mayonnaise. Spread sardine filling on 6 slices of bread. Top with lettuce, if desired, and remaining 6 slices of bread. Serves 6.

Sardine and Cheese Sandwich

>   4 slices rye bread, toasted
>   Butter
>   2 3¾-ounce cans sardines in oil, drained
>   ⅓ cup chili sauce
>   2 tablespoons chopped onion
>   2 ounces process American cheese, shredded (½ cup)

Spread toasted bread with butter. Arrange sardines on toast. Combine chili sauce and onion; spoon over sardines. Place on baking sheet and bake at 450° for 10 minutes. Top with shredded cheese. Return to oven and heat just till cheese melts. Makes 4 sandwiches.

SARSAPARILLA (*sär suh puh ril' uh, sär spuh-, sas' puh-*)—A soft drink flavored with the dried roots of a tropical American climbing plant related to the lily.

SASSAFRAS—A tree of the laurel family, native to America. The powdered leaves are used to make filé powder. This powder typically is used to thicken and season gumbos and stews in Creole cookery. Because of their bitey and spicy flavor, the bark and roots are used in flavoring sassafras tea and other beverages, and as one of the ingredients in root beer.

SATSUMA—A mandarin orange variety. (See also *Mandarin Orange*.)

SAUCE

Master the art of saucemaking, and turn any dish into a glamorous treat.

A sauce is the crowning glory of any dish with which it is served. This liquid or semiliquid blend of ingredients not only adds flavor but it enhances the appearance of foods. The sauce should complement, contrast, and cling to the food on which or beside which it is served.

Tracing the origins of sauce is a difficult task, as is the case with many other foods. The word sauce evolved from the Latin word *salsus* (salted), and it is known that the early Greeks and Romans used sauces on their foods. Whether or not sauces were used earlier than this is, at best, only conjecture.

During medieval times in England, people did not think highly of simple dishes. To overcome this stigma, they added a sauce. These early sauces consisted of either a heavy gravy made by boiling down meat stock or a sweet mixture of honey or sugar, vinegar, and spices.

Sauces remained relatively simple creations until the seventeenth and eighteenth centuries when French chefs added a new dimension to the art of saucemaking. These inventive men transformed simple sauces into classic ones by adding other ingredients, such as herbs, eggs, vegetables, and cheeses. Many of the now-famous sauces were developed in the kitchens of French nobility. Kings generously rewarded chefs who created new sauces. Then, as now, being the sauce chef in a kitchen was an important duty.

Tantalizing seafood sauces

← Choose Jiffy Hollandaise (see *Hollandaise* for recipe)—top; Easy Seafood Sauce—middle; Tartar Sauce Deluxe—bottom; or Clarified Butter to top off seafood dishes.

The names given to the sauces created during this period often indicated the origin of the particular sauce. For example, Béarnaise was named for a region in southwestern France called Béarn. Béchamel was named for Louis de Béchamel, head steward of the kitchen in which the meals of Louis XIV were prepared. Another sauce, mayonnaise, named for the town of Mahon on the Spanish island of Minorca, was first made for the Duc de Richelieu; and the famous sauce, Bordelaise, was named after the Bordeaux region of France.

Basic ingredients: A sauce is only as good as the ingredients you put into it *and* the care you take when preparing it. Basic ingredients for sauces include cream, milk, stock, or wine for the liquid; butter for richness; eggs, flour, bread or starch for thickening; and herbs, spices, vegetables, and fruits for flavor.

While it's important to use the kinds of ingredients called for to duplicate a sauce, you can add your own creative touch by experimenting with flavor ingredients such as herbs rather than changing the basic ingredients.

To simplify saucemaking, make full use of the many high-quality, ready-to-use ingredients, mixes, and bottled and canned products that are available in the supermarket. Some of the bottled products, such as hot pepper sauce, Worcestershire sauce, and chili sauce, can be used as the base for many other sauces.

A few of the traditional bottled meat sauces have been on the market for generations. Today, they are joined by Hollandaise and Bordelaise, as well as various dessert or sundae sauces and sauces for use on pasta and meats. With

Know Your Classic Sauces		
Names of Sauces	Basic Ingredients	Characteristic Ingredients
White Sauces		
Béchamel Sauce* (classic White Sauce)	white roux, milk	
Caper Sauce	"	capers
Egg Sauce*	"	hard-cooked egg
Mornay Sauce (Cheese Sauce)	"	cheese, cream
Nantua Sauce	"	crayfish butter, cream
Raifort Sauce	"	horseradish
Soubise Sauce	"	puréed onion
Véronique	"	cream, white grapes
Velouté Sauce*	white roux; chicken, fish, or veal stock	
Allemande* or Parisienne Sauce	"	cream, egg yolks
Bercy Sauce (Shallot Sauce)	"	shallots, white wine, veal or fish stock to thin
Brown Sauces		
Espagnole Sauce	browned roux, white wine, meat stock	carrot, onion, celery, bouquet garni, tomato sauce or purée
Demi-Glaze Sauce	"	cooked down to concentrate
Bordelaise Sauce*	"	red wine (Bordeaux), garlic, shallots
Chasseur Sauce (Hunter's Sauce)	"	mushrooms, shallots, white wine, tomato
Diable* (Deviled Sauce)	"	Worcestershire sauce, vinegar, white wine
Duxelles Sauce	"	mushrooms, white wine, tomato
Emulsified Sauces		
Hollandaise Sauce* (cooked)	egg yolks, butter, lemon juice or vinegar	
Béarnaise Sauce*	"	shallots, tarragon, vinegar, white wine
Mousseline Sauce*	"	whipped cream folded in
Mayonnaise* (uncooked)	egg yolks, oil, lemon juice or vinegar	
Aïoli Sauce	"	garlic
Rémoulade Sauce	"	mustard, gherkins, capers, parsley, herbs
Tartar Sauce*	"	herbs, pickles, onions
Vinaigrette Sauces		
Basic Vinaigrette* (Clear French Dressing)	vinegar, oil	herbs and seasonings
*See also individual listings.		

all of the convenience products that are available on the market, there is little excuse for doing without a sauced food.

Remember that the sauce on a food is usually the first thing to touch your tongue. Always put a good sauce on good food, as this will enhance the food's taste appeal. However, a good sauce does little to make a poor food taste better.

Types of sauces

The art of saucemaking that has developed over the years stems from the classic sauce types, often referred to as the "mother sauces." These sauces include the white sauces—Béchamel and Velouté; Espagnole or Brown Sauce; two basic emulsified sauces—Hollandaise and Mayonnaise; and Vinaigrette or oil and vinegar sauces. When you prepare sauces, you use endless variations of these basic sauce types. In addition, these classic sauces have been joined by modern-day dessert sauces, sundae sauces, barbecue and brush-on sauces, and a wide variety of gravies.

The method of preparing the various types of sauces incorporates some of the same techniques. For example, a roux is basic to many of the white and brown sauces. This cooked mixture of flour and butter is an important contribution to the saucemaking art. (See also *Roux*.)

The classic white sauce is often known as cream sauce because of its appearance. It is the king of all sauces in the United States and is probably used most frequently in all types of dishes. As can be seen on the Know Your Classic Sauces chart, many different sauces start out as basic white sauce. (See also *White Sauce*.)

Brown sauces are also starch-thickened. However, the fat-flour roux is browned before the other ingredients are added. There are also variations of this classic type as seen on the chart.

Hollandaise and Mayonnaise are two sauces that are made with an emulsion of egg yolks and fat. These emulsified sauces have several variations, too.

Vinaigrette sauces are a simple blend of oil, vinegar, salt, and pepper, and actually are a clear French salad dressing.

Creamy Mustard Sauce (see *Egg* for recipe) adds both flavor and color contrast to broccoli, other green vegetables, or ham loaf.

A simplified version of white sauce makes use of an electric blender and eliminates the step of making the roux. The blender can also be used for bread sauce, a bread-thickened white sauce.

Blender White Sauce

Thin:
    1 cup milk
    1 tablespoon all-purpose flour
    1 tablespoon butter or margarine
Medium:
    1 cup milk
    2 tablespoons all-purpose flour
    2 tablespoons butter or margarine
Thick:
    1 cup milk
    ¼ cup all-purpose flour
    3 tablespoons butter or margarine

Put milk, flour, butter, and ¼ teaspoon salt in blender container; blend smooth. In saucepan cook and stir till bubbly. Makes 1 cup.

Bread Sauce

    1 **cup hot milk**
    2 **tablespoons butter or margarine**
   1/4 **teaspoon salt**
     White bread, crusts removed*

Warm blender container by filling with hot water and letting stand a minute or two; empty water. Put hot milk, butter or margarine, and salt in blender container; blend till ingredients are mixed. With blender running, break bread into pieces and add to blender container. Stop blender occasionally to check sauce consistency. Serve at once. Makes 1¼ cups.

    *Use 3 to 4 slices of bread for thin sauce, 6 to 7 slices of bread for medium sauce, and 9 to 10 slices of bread for thick sauce. Unless a white-colored sauce is desired, leave the bread crusts on and use less bread.

Sauce success tips

● Stir constantly while starch-thickened sauces cook to prevent lumping. If you must leave the sauce for a few seconds, set the pan off the heat during that time.

● If the starch-thickened sauce develops a few lumps, beat them out with a rotary beater or a wire whisk. As a last resort, strain sauce with sieve to remove lumps.

● Cook egg-thickened sauces over low heat, preferably using a controlled-heat burner or element. Or cook these sauces in the top of a double boiler over hot, not boiling, water. First, warm the egg yolks by stirring in a little of the hot sauce mixture. Then add to the remainder of the sauce mixture. Never let a sauce boil after the egg yolks are added. Sauce may curdle.

● Don't let water boil in the bottom of the double boiler if you use it to make a custard sauce. Also, make sure the water doesn't touch bottom of pan holding custard.

● Mayonnaise or mayonnaise-based sauces, such as Tartar Sauce, may separate if put on very hot foods. Pass the sauce after the food reaches the table and has cooled a bit.

● To make sauces with a rich color, add Kitchen Bouquet to gravies or yellow food coloring to cream sauces made with egg.

Mayonnaise is the basic for a gamut of cold sauces. One of the most famous of these is Tartar Sauce, a seafood favorite.

Blender Tartar Sauce

    1 **cup mayonnaise or salad dressing**
    1 **tablespoon lemon juice**
    1 **large dill pickle, cut in pieces**
   1/4 **small onion**
    1 **hard-cooked egg, quartered**
    1 **tablespoon capers, drained**
    1 **teaspoon snipped chives**

Put all ingredients in blender container; blend till ingredients are chopped. Chill thoroughly. Serve with fish. Makes 2 cups.

Tartar Sauce Deluxe

   1/2 **cup dairy sour cream**
   1/4 **cup mayonnaise or salad dressing**
    1 **hard-cooked egg, chopped**
    2 **tablespoons pickle relish**
    2 **tablespoons chopped green onion**
    2 **tablespoons sauterne**
      ● ● ●
     Sieved egg yolk
     Sliced green onion

Blend together the sour cream, mayonnaise or salad dressing, chopped hard-cooked egg, pickle relish, chopped green onion, and sauterne. Chill the mixture thoroughly. Garnish top of sauce with sieved egg yolk and sliced green onion. Makes 1½ cups sauce.

Some of the other sauces that, strictly speaking, don't fit under the previous categories include marinades, basting sauces, sauces that coat the food as an integral part of the mixture, some types of fruit sauces, and pan gravies.

An elegant candlelight dinner

The sauce for Creamy Ham Rolls, a conve- →
nient main dish, starts with a mix to which frozen onions in cream sauce are added.

Instead of serving plain fried chicken, try Chicken with Orange Rice, which features pieces of chicken with a currant-orange sauce. You'll also find sunny orange flavor in the rice.

Burgundy Sauce

½ cup salad oil
½ cup Burgundy *or* claret
2 tablespoons finely snipped candied ginger
2 tablespoons catsup
2 tablespoons molasses
1 large clove garlic, minced
½ teaspoon curry powder
½ teaspoon salt
½ teaspoon pepper

Combine all ingredients. Use as a marinade or basting sauce for barbecued meat. Makes 1 cup.

Tangy Cranberry Sauce

Mix one 16-ounce can jellied cranberry sauce, ⅓ cup bottled steak sauce, 1 tablespoon *each* brown sugar and salad oil, and 2 teaspoons prepared mustard. Beat with rotary beater. Serve warm or as is with ham or pork. Makes 2 cups.

Think of sauces as both complementing and contrasting the food on which or beside which they are served. Hollandaise, for example, contrasts in color and texture, and complements in flavor a vegetable such as broccoli. The sharp seasoning of barbecue sauce cuts the richness of spareribs, while the colors of the meat and the sauce blend together attractively.

Light sauce can be used on light foods, but there should be a subtle difference of shading. Pale golden cheese sauce, for instance, is more appealing on macaroni than the best flavored white sauce ever could be. Milk chocolate sauce looks better on vanilla or coffee ice cream than on chocolate ice cream which has the same brown shade, but deep-colored fudge sauce on chocolate ice cream is perfect.

When you sauce a food, use a light hand. Don't use so much that the food is masked, but let some of the food show through. Or, for a change, put the sauce beside rather than on top of the food. Serve the sauce attractively, then pass around the remaining for seconds.

Sauces can be used on any type of food, no matter whether it's a main dish, a vegetable, or a dessert.

Main-dish sauces: Add a spark of additional flavor to main dishes. Flavorwise, some sauces go better with one type of meat than with another. For example, mint and dill are naturals with lamb, while mustard, cheese, or cherries are partners with ham. Poultry and fruit go together like steak and mushrooms or seafood and mayonnaise or butter sauces.

Chicken with Orange Rice

½ cup currant jelly
¼ cup frozen orange juice
　　concentrate
2 teaspoons cornstarch
1 teaspoon dry mustard
　　Dash bottled hot pepper sauce
　　　• • •
½ cup all-purpose flour
1 teaspoon salt
1 2½- to 3-pound ready-to-cook
　　broiler-fryer chicken, cut up
　　Shortening
　　Orange Rice

Combine jelly, orange juice concentrate, and ⅓ cup water; cook and stir till smooth. Blend cornstarch, mustard, hot pepper sauce, and 1 tablespoon cold water; stir into jelly mixture. Cook and stir till thickened; set aside. Combine flour and salt in paper bag. Add 2 or 3 pieces of chicken at a time; shake to coat. Brown chicken in hot shortening, turning occasionally. Drain excess fat; add the currant-orange sauce. Cover; simmer over low heat till tender, 45 minutes. Baste occasionally with sauce. Serve with Orange Rice. Serves 4.

Orange Rice: Cook 1 cup chopped celery and ¼ cup chopped onion in ¼ cup butter till tender. Add 2 tablespoons frozen orange juice concentrate, 1¼ cups water, and ½ teaspoon salt. Bring the mixture to boiling. Add 1⅓ cups uncooked packaged precooked rice. Continue cooking as directed on the package.

Bacon-wrapped Lamb Patties with Dill Sauce will delight lamb lovers. The creamy sauce combines dill and Parmesan flavors.

Lamb Patties with Dill Sauce

1 beaten egg
½ cup quick-cooking rolled oats
¼ cup finely chopped onion
1 teaspoon salt
¼ teaspoon dried thyme leaves,
　　crushed
　　Dash pepper
1½ pounds ground lamb
6 slices bacon
　　Dill Sauce

Combine egg, oats, onion, salt, thyme, and pepper. Add lamb and mix well. Shape mixture into 6 patties. Wrap each patty with 1 slice bacon; secure with wooden pick. Broil 5 inches from heat for 10 minutes. Turn; broil 5 minutes longer. Serve with Dill Sauce. Serves 6.

Dill Sauce: Cook 1 tablespoon finely chopped onion in 1 tablespoon butter or margarine till tender. Blend in 2 tablespoons all-purpose flour, 2 tablespoons grated Parmesan cheese, ½ teaspoon dried dillweed, ½ teaspoon paprika, and dash salt. Add 1 cup milk all at once. Cook and stir till thickened and bubbly.

Fresh Mint Sauce

Combine ¼ cup snipped, fresh mint leaves, ¼ cup light corn syrup, and 1 tablespoon lemon juice. Blend together ¼ cup water and 1½ teaspoons cornstarch; add to mint mixture. Cook and stir over medium heat till thickened and bubbly; strain. Stir in 1 drop green food coloring. Serve with lamb. Makes ½ cup sauce.

In-a-Hurry Mint Sauce

Combine ½ cup mint jelly and 2 teaspoons lemon juice. Heat slowly, stirring occasionally, till jelly melts. Serve with lamb. Makes ½ cup.

Creamy Ham Rolls

> 1 12-ounce package frozen rice with peas and mushrooms
> 2 ounces sharp process American cheese, shredded (½ cup)
> 8 slices boiled ham
> 1 10-ounce package frozen onions in cream sauce
> 1 envelope white sauce mix

Prepare frozen rice according to package directions. (Omit Parmesan cheese if called for.) Stir in American cheese; spoon about ¼ *cup* mixture on each ham slice. Roll up jelly-roll fashion. Prepare frozen onions in cream sauce according to package directions.

In blazer pan of large chafing dish, prepare white sauce mix over direct heat following package directions. Add cooked onions with cream sauce. Arrange ham rolls in sauce. Cover and heat through. Makes 4 servings.

Hot Mustard Sauce

In saucepan melt 3 tablespoons butter or margarine; blend in 1 teaspoon all-purpose flour. Add ¼ cup vinegar, ¼ cup beef broth, ¼ cup prepared horseradish mustard, and 3 tablespoons brown sugar. Cook slowly, stirring constantly, till thickened. Gradually add a little hot mixture to 1 slightly beaten egg yolk; return to hot mixture. Bring sauce just to boiling point, stirring constantly; serve hot with corned beef or ham. Makes 1 cup.

Spicy Cherry Sauce

> ¾ cup sugar
> Dash salt
> 2 tablespoons cornstarch
> ¾ cup orange juice
> 1 tablespoon lemon juice
> 1 16-ounce can pitted, tart red cherries (water pack)
> 1 1-inch stick cinnamon
> ½ teaspoon whole cloves
> ¼ teaspoon red food coloring

Combine sugar, salt, and cornstarch. Stir in orange and lemon juices. Add undrained cherries, spices, and food coloring. Cook, stirring constantly, over medium heat till mixture thickens and comes to a boil. Boil 2 minutes. Before serving, remove the cinnamon and cloves. Serve warm with ham. Makes 3 cups.

1-2-3 Sauce

Combine one 12-ounce bottle extra-hot catsup, 2 teaspoons celery seed, 3 tablespoons vinegar, and 1 clove garlic, halved. Chill several hours; remove garlic before serving. Grill hamburgers a few minutes on each side, then baste with sauce. Makes 1¼ cups sauce.

Wine-Mushroom Sauce

Cook 1 cup sliced fresh mushrooms and ¼ cup finely chopped green onion in ¼ cup butter till tender. Blend in 4 teaspoons cornstarch. Add ¾ cup Burgundy, ¾ cup water, 2 tablespoons snipped parsley, ¾ teaspoon salt, and dash pepper. Cook and stir till thickened and bubbly. Serve with steak. Makes 1½ cups.

Easy Seafood Sauce

> ½ cup mayonnaise or salad dressing
> 3 tablespoons catsup
> 1 teaspoon prepared horseradish
> ¼ teaspoon garlic salt
> Snipped parsley

Combine mayonnaise, catsup, horseradish, and garlic salt; blend together. Chill thoroughly. Sprinkle with snipped parsley. Makes ¾ cup.

Clarified Butter

Melt butter over low heat without stirring; cool. Pour off oily top layer; discard bottom layer. Keep butter warm over candle warmer. Serve with steamed or poached fish or shellfish.

Vegetable sauces: Spoon a creamy or buttery sauce over garden-fresh vegetables. The smooth sauce contrasts in texture and at the same time gives an added flavor that's hard to beat. Cheese sauces are good accompaniments for vegetables, as are herbed butter sauces or creamy sauces delicately flavored with mustard.

Blue Cheese Sauce

      2 tablespoons butter or margarine
      2 tablespoons all-purpose flour
      1 chicken bouillon cube
      1 cup milk
    ¼ cup dairy sour cream
    ¼ cup crumbled blue cheese

In saucepan melt butter; stir in flour. Add crushed bouillon cube and milk all at once. Cook, stirring constantly, till mixture thickens and bubbles. Remove from heat; stir in sour cream and blue cheese. Heat through, *but do not boil*. Serve with baked potatoes or green vegetables. Makes 1¼ cups sauce.

Fix a quick sundae sauce by simply combining butter-toasted nuts and a milk chocolate bar. Complete the sundae by spooning warm Chocolate-Walnut Sauce over chocolate ripple ice cream.

Parmesan Cheese Sauce

1 tablespoon butter or margarine
1 tablespoon all-purpose flour
¼ teaspoon salt
Dash pepper
Dash paprika
Dash dry mustard
1 cup milk
2 tablespoons grated Parmesan
cheese
2 tablespoons toasted, slivered
almonds

In saucepan melt butter; stir in flour, salt, pepper, paprika, and dry mustard. Add milk all at once. Cook and stir till sauce thickens and bubbles. Add cheese and almonds; stir the mixture till cheese melts. Serve over drained, cooked vegetables. Makes 1 cup sauce.

Sour Cream Sauce

Combine ½ cup dairy sour cream, 2 tablespoons salad dressing, 2 teaspoons chopped green onion, 1½ teaspoons lemon juice, ½ teaspoon sugar, ¼ teaspoon dry mustard, and dash salt. Heat mixture, stirring constantly, till warm, *but do not boil*. Makes ½ cup sauce.

Dessert sauces: Top off dessert foods, such as puddings, cakes, ice cream, or fruits, with a luscious sauce. Classic examples of dessert sauces include brandy, foamy, or hard sauces spooned over warm plum puddings and spice cakes. Ice cream sauces can be as simple as fudge or mint sauce purchased at the store, or as elegant as Cherries Jubilee or other fruit sauces served over various flavors of ice cream or sherbet. A favorite sauce for fruit desserts is a creamy custard sauce.

Cherry Sundae Sauce

Combine ½ cup sugar and 2 teaspoons cornstarch. Add to 2 cups quartered, fresh dark sweet cherries in a saucepan. Heat and stir till sugar dissolves and mixture thickens slightly. Stir in 1 tablespoon lemon juice. Chill. Serve over ice cream. Makes 1⅔ cups sauce.

Fruit Sparkle Sauce

1 30-ounce can fruit cocktail
¼ cup sugar
1 tablespoon cornstarch
¼ teaspoon salt
¼ cup water
½ 6-ounce can frozen orange juice
concentrate, thawed
(⅓ cup)
¼ cup coarsely chopped pecans

Drain fruit cocktail, reserving syrup. In a saucepan combine sugar, cornstarch, and salt; blend in water. Add syrup and orange juice concentrate. Cook and stir till mixture thickens and boils. Add drained fruit cocktail; chill. Stir in pecans. Serve the sauce over vanilla ice cream. Makes 3½ cups sauce.

Tropical Sundae Sauce

1 8¾-ounce can pineapple tidbits
1½ cups sugar
1½ tablespoons lemon juice
3 drops peppermint extract
2 medium oranges, peeled,
sectioned, and seeded
½ cup green maraschino cherries,
halved

Drain pineapple, reserving syrup; add enough water to syrup to make ½ cup. In a saucepan cook sugar and syrup over low heat till thickened, about 12 minutes. Add lemon juice and peppermint extract; chill. Before serving the sauce, add oranges and cherries. Serve over vanilla ice cream. Makes 2 cups sauce.

Hot Fudge–Peanut Butter Sauce

1 6-ounce package semisweet
chocolate pieces
1 cup milk
½ cup sugar
½ cup peanut butter

In small saucepan combine chocolate, milk, and sugar. Bring to boiling, stirring constantly. Gradually stir chocolate mixture into peanut butter. Ladle warm sauce atop ice cream or over pound cake a la mode. Makes 2 cups.

Fruit sauce over fruit is the main theme for this fancy dessert called Bananas aux Fruits. Crumb-coated bananas are baked with an apricot mixture, then topped with cherry-wine sauce.

Bananas aux Fruits

 1 slightly beaten egg
 1 tablespoon lemon juice
 6 firm, medium-sized bananas
 9 soft macaroon cookies
 2 tablespoons all-purpose flour
¼ cup apricot preserves
 2 tablespoons butter, melted
 2 teaspoons lemon juice
   Cherry Sauce

Combine egg and 1 tablespoon lemon juice. Peel bananas and coat with egg mixture; place on greased baking sheet. Break cookies into coarse crumbs (1½ cups); stir in flour and pile mixture on bananas. Bake at 375° for 8 to 10 minutes. Combine preserves, butter, and 2 teaspoons lemon juice. Spoon over bananas. Bake till hot, 3 to 5 minutes more. Serve with hot Cherry Sauce. Makes 6 servings.

Cherry Sauce: Drain one 8¾-ounce can pitted dark sweet cherries, reserving syrup. Halve cherries. Add enough port wine to syrup to make ¾ cup. In saucepan combine 2 tablespoons sugar, 1 tablespoon cornstarch, and dash salt. Stir in reserved syrup mixture. Cook, stirring constantly, till mixture thickens and bubbles. Add cherries and heat just to boiling.

Chocolate–Walnut Sauce

¼ cup butter or margarine
½ cup coarsely chopped walnuts
 1 4½-ounce milk chocolate bar,
   broken in pieces

In heavy skillet melt butter. Add nuts; cook and stir over medium heat till nuts are toasted. Add chocolate; stir till melted and smooth. Serve warm over ice cream. Makes 1 cup.

SAUCE BOAT—A serving dish shaped like a low, oval pitcher with a pouring lip. A plate or tray is often attached at the bottom to catch drips. Larger sizes with attached trays are called gravy boats.

SAUCEPAN—A cooking pot that ranges in capacity from one cup to four quarts and has a handle. Most types are deep in proportion to width and have a flat bottom, straight or slightly sloping sides, and a tight-fitting cover. Saucepans are made of plain metal, porcelain-coated metal, glass ceramic, or heatproof glass. These utensils are used for boiling, simmering, and stewing foods as well as for making sauces. (See also *Pots and Pans*.)

SAUCISSON *(sō sē sôn')*—The French word for a large, smoked, pork sausage.

SAUERBRATEN *(sour'brät'uhn)* German-style beef pot roast that is marinated and cooked in a vinegar mixture. The cooking liquid is often thickened, usually with gingersnaps, and served with the meat.

Sauerbraten

  2 medium onions, sliced
  ½ lemon, sliced
1½ cups red wine vinegar
12 whole cloves
  6 bay leaves
  6 whole peppercorns
  1 tablespoon sugar
  ¼ teaspoon ground ginger
  1 4-pound beef rump roast
  2 tablespoons shortening
    Gravy

In large bowl or crock combine first 8 ingredients, 2½ cups water, and 1 tablespoon salt. Add roast, turning to coat. Cover and refrigerate about 36 hours; turn meat several times. Remove meat; wipe dry. Strain; reserve marinade. In Dutch oven, brown meat in hot shortening; add strained marinade. Cover and cook slowly till tender, about 2 hours. Remove meat. Serve with Gravy. Makes 10 servings.

Gravy: For each cup of gravy combine ¾ cup meat juices and ¼ cup water; add ⅓ cup broken gingersnaps. Cook and stir till thick.

SAUERKRAUT, KRAUT *(sour' krout', sou' uhr-)*—Shredded cabbage that is fermented in a brine of salt and cabbage juice. The brine serves the double purpose of preserving the cabbage and giving it the sour flavor that accounts for the name, literally "sour cabbage."

The people of the Orient first made sauerkraut several thousand years ago. Much later, during the thirteenth century, invading Tartars introduced this dish to eastern Europe. The people of this area, particularly the Germans, soon became so fond of sauerkraut that even today it is associated with this area.

In Germany, you'll not only find the world-famous sauerkraut but also sauerkraut and sausage, sauerkraut cooked with fruit such as pineapple, sauerkraut cooked in beer or wine, and sauerkraut seasoned with spices. However, sauerkraut is not limited to Germany; it is enjoyed in all parts of the world.

Some homemakers still make their own sauerkraut, but today, most sauerkraut is packed commercially. Even though the commercial operations involve tremendous quantities of raw materials, the technique for making sauerkraut has changed very little in the past several centuries. Basically, cabbage and salt are layered in a deep container, and this mixture is pounded to start release of the juice. Then, the mixture is allowed to ferment. After several weeks, the sauerkraut has developed a full flavor and is ready to be eaten fresh or packed.

Although the flavor of fresh sauerkraut is quite mild, older sauerkraut is apt to have a strong flavor that is objectionable to some people. To tame this flavor, rinse the sauerkraut several times with cold water before cooking it.

The flavor alone is enough to make many people enjoy sauerkraut, but when you also consider that 1 cup of drained sauerkraut has only about 30 calories, this vegetable becomes enticing to weight watchers. Sauerkraut also has vitamin C and other vitamins and minerals.

The flavor of heated sauerkraut blends well with pork products and sausages. Corned beef and sauerkraut are a popular combination in a Reuben sandwich. Cold sauerkraut is delicious in salads or as a relish. Also try sauerkraut in combination with other meats, poultry, and vegetables, and remember that sauerkraut juice adds flavor to vegetable juice cocktails.

Frankrauts

Using 1 pound frankfurters, slit frankfurters lengthwise *not quite through*. Lightly brush cut surfaces with liquid smoke. Combine 1 cup drained sauerkraut, ¼ cup chili sauce, and 1 teaspoon caraway seed; stuff franks. Wrap *each* stuffed frank with a strip of partially cooked bacon; use wooden picks to hold bacon in place. Grill over *hot* coals, turning occasionally, 10 to 15 minutes. Serves 4 or 5.

Quick Frank-Kraut Dinner

    ¼ cup milk
    1 10¾-ounce can condensed
        Cheddar cheese soup
    ½ teaspoon caraway seed
    ½ teaspoon prepared mustard
    1 27-ounce can sauerkraut,
        drained and snipped
    1 pound frankfurters (8 to 10)

Gradually stir milk into cheese soup till well blended; add caraway seed and mustard. Fold in sauerkraut; heat through, stirring frequently. Turn into a 10x6x1½-inch baking dish. Slash each frankfurter diagonally at 1-inch intervals; arrange frankfurters atop sauerkraut mixture. Bake at 375° till frankfurters are heated through, 15 to 20 minutes. Serves 4.

Sausage-Potato Skillet

Using 1 package dry scalloped potatoes, combine dry potatoes and the packaged seasoned sauce mix. Add water to potatoes to equal *total liquid* called for on package. Heat to boiling; stir occasionally. Reduce heat; simmer, covered, till potatoes are tender, 30 minutes. Stir in one 16-ounce can sauerkraut, drained; sprinkle with ½ teaspoon caraway seed. Arrange 1 pound smoked pork sausage links, spoke-fashion, on top of mixture. Cover, cook about 10 minutes more. Serves 4 to 6.

Cut Sauerbraten into thick slices and serve it with Potato Pancakes (see *Kartoffel Pfannkuchen* for recipe) for a delectable meal.

Frank and Kraut Stew

A hearty stew—

    1 large onion, sliced (1 cup)
    ½ cup chopped green pepper
    2 tablespoons shortening
    1 16-ounce can sauerkraut
    1 16-ounce can tomatoes
    3 potatoes, peeled and cubed
    2 medium carrots, thinly sliced
        (about ½ cup)
    ½ cup water
    2 tablespoons brown sugar
    1 teaspoon salt
    ¼ teaspoon pepper
    1 pound frankfurters, quartered

In Dutch oven or large skillet cook sliced onion and chopped green pepper in shortening till tender. Add sauerkraut, tomatoes, potatoes, carrots, water, brown sugar, salt, and pepper. Simmer, covered, till vegetables are tender, about 35 minutes. Add frankfurters; simmer 10 minutes longer. Makes 5 or 6 servings.

Spareribs with Kraut

> 3 pounds pork spareribs
> 2 teaspoons salt
> ¼ teaspoon pepper
> 1 27-ounce can sauerkraut
> 1 cup finely chopped, unpeeled,
>   tart apple
> 1 cup shredded carrot
> 1½ cups tomato juice
> 2 tablespoons brown sugar
> 2 teaspoons caraway seed

Cut ribs in pieces; season with salt and pepper; place in Dutch oven and brown well. Combine sauerkraut (including liquid) with chopped apple, shredded carrot, tomato juice, brown sugar, and the 2 teaspoons caraway seed; spoon over ribs. Simmer, covered, till the ribs are done, about 1¾ hours; baste with juices several times during the last hour of cooking. Skim off excess fat. Makes 6 servings.

Place prebrowned meatballs atop the sauerkraut-rice mixture for Meatball-Sauerkraut Skillet. Then, add tomatoes and cook.

Sauerkraut Provençale

An unusual vegetable dish—

> ⅓ cup chopped onion
> 2 tablespoons butter or margarine,
>   melted
> ⅓ cup canned condensed beef broth
> 1 14-ounce can sauerkraut,
>   drained
> 2 tablespoons chopped, canned
>   pimiento
>   •   •   •
> ½ cup dairy sour cream
>   Poppy seed

Cook chopped onion in melted butter or margarine till tender but not brown. Add condensed beef broth, drained sauerkraut, and chopped pimiento; mix lightly. Simmer, covered, for 10 minutes. Serve topped with dairy sour cream and dashed with poppy seed. Makes 4 servings.

Meatball-Sauerkraut Skillet

A tasty combination—

> 1 pound ground beef
> 3 cups soft bread crumbs
>   (3 to 4 slices bread)
> ¼ cup milk
> 1 egg
> ¾ teaspoon salt
>   Dash pepper
> 2 tablespoons shortening
>   •   •   •
> 1 27-ounce can sauerkraut,
>   drained
> ½ cup chopped onion
> ½ teaspoon salt
> ¾ cup uncooked long-grain rice
> 1½ cups water
> 1 16-ounce can tomatoes, cut up

In bowl combine ground beef, bread crumbs, milk, egg, ¾ teaspoon salt, and pepper. Mix well. Shape into 12 meatballs. Brown in shortening in large skillet; remove meatballs.

In same skillet combine drained sauerkraut, chopped onion, and ½ teaspoon salt. Stir in uncooked rice and water. Add meatballs and tomatoes. Bring to boiling; reduce heat and simmer, covered, for 30 to 35 minutes. Serves 6.

SAUSAGE—A general name for over 200 meat products made of chopped or ground, seasoned meat and frequently stuffed into casings. Sausages are prepared from beef, veal, pork, lamb, liver, poultry, or a mixture of meats that are flavored with spices and herbs, and can be processed by salting, pickling, or smoking. The variety of sausages available includes mild, hot, moist, and dry sausages as well as thick or thin tubes, small or large links, and even loose sausage meat.

Federal regulations specify the ingredients, including the amount of fat and the additives that are used in each kind of sausage. For example, pork sausage can contain up to 50 percent fat, while frankfurters are limited to 30 percent.

Sausage has been used for such a long time that it is thought that a caveman was probably responsible for discovering how to preserve meat by hanging it over the smoke and heat of a fire or by letting it dry in the sun. As man became more sophisticated in his food habits, it was found that curing and then smoking meats improved keeping quality. It is known that sausagelike meats were prepared and eaten by the ancient Babylonians and the Chinese more than a thousand years before the Christian Era.

In 900 B.C., Homer wrote of a sort of sausage in the Odyssey. Other ancient Greeks also referred to sausage in their plays, and one writer about 500 B.C. spoke of salami, a sausage named for the ancient city of Salamis on Cyprus.

The Romans called sausage meats *salsus*, meaning salted. One of their specialties was made of fresh pork, pine nuts, cumin, bay leaves, and pepper.

By the Middle Ages, sausagemaking was a flourishing business. Sausagemakers wisely used the meats and seasonings that were plentiful in their regions. This practice resulted in distinctive sausages that were famous throughout Europe. Many of these local sausages carried with them the name of the city of their origin—Bologna sausage and Genoa salami. In some countries, sausages contained other foods of the area mixed with the meat, such as oatmeal in Scotland and cabbage in Luxembourg.

The popular pair, frankfurters and sauerkraut, combine in a delicious way in this easy-to-make Frank and Kraut Stew.

When early settlers arrived in America, they found the Indians making a sausage of chopped dried beef and berries. As people came from different countries to live in the New World, they brought their knowledge of making European-type sausages. Soon, some local, community sausage kitchens began to duplicate the homemakers' recipes commercially.

As the years passed new types of sausages were invented, too. One of these, scrapple, a mixture of pork, cornmeal, and spices cooked together and then shaped into a loaf, was created by the thrifty Pennsylvania Dutch to use up every bit of meat after butchering a hog.

Nutritional value: Like all meats, sausage is a source of high-quality protein, vitamins, and minerals. However, since the ingredients in different sausages vary greatly, the amount of these nutrients in sausage depends on the kind of sausage. The caloric value of sausage also depends on the kind of sausage. For example, three cooked, brown-and-serve sausages yield about 280 calories. The same portion of bologna provides 130 calories.

How sausage is manufactured: Although the recipes and some of the processing steps for sausage vary depending on the type of sausage being made and who's making it, there are several processes that are used in making any sausage.

The very important first step in making sausage is chopping or grinding and mixing the sausage ingredients. This is accomplished quickly by large, high-speed machines. Interestingly, in the making of some sausages, ice or cold water (the amount is regulated by law) is added to the mixture during the chopping process. This not only lowers the mixture to the proper temperature, but it also facilitates the mixing of seasonings and helps to control the texture of the sausage.

The next step in making most sausages is the stuffing process. Again, large machines are used. First, the sausage mixture is packed into the machine as tightly as possible to eliminate air pockets from forming. Then, the machine stuffs the meat mixture into either natural or cellulose casings of various diameters.

Since the sausage is in a very long tube when it leaves the stuffing machine, it is next sent to the linking machine, which twists or ties off the sausage into shorter lengths. The length of each sausage link depends on the type of sausage. Although most sausages are eventually cut into individual links, usually the links are left hooked together until later.

The smokehouse is the next stop in sausage processing. Originally, sausage was smoked to preserve it, but today refrigeration takes care of preservation. The smoking now is done for flavoring. The hardwood sawdust used, the amount of smoke, and the length of time the sausage is smoked differ, depending on the type of sausage, but all are carefully controlled to produce the desired flavor.

Sausages that are ready to eat when purchased have either been cooked or dried during processing. If the cooked sausages are also to be smoked, the two processes are often combined by cooking the sausage in the smokehouse. However, sausages may also be cooked with separate hot water or steam equipment. Dry sausages undergo two special processes—fermentation and drying. Fermentation is responsible for the tangy flavor of dry sausages, and the controlled air-drying of these sausages makes them ready to eat without cooking.

Types of sausages: Depending on their processing, sausages are grouped into one of five types—fresh; uncooked; smoked; cooked, smoked; and dry.

Fresh sausage is made by seasoning uncured, fresh meat, usually pork or beef. All fresh sausages, such as fresh pork sausage, bratwurst, weisswurst, and bockwurst, must be cooked.

The second type of sausage—uncooked, smoked sausage made from cured meat—also requires cooking by the homemaker. This type includes country-style pork sausage, linguisa, and mettwurst.

Sausages classed as cooked sausages are usually made from uncured meat, but cured meat is sometimes used. After stuffing, these sausages are thoroughly cooked in special hot water or steam cooking equipment. Blood sausage, liver sausage, and blood and tongue sausage are examples of this type of sausage. Often, these fully cooked sausages are served cold, but they may be heated.

The two most popular kinds of sausages, frankfurters and bologna, are both cooked, smoked sausages as are Berliner sausage, Polish sausage, knackwurst, and smokie links. Cured meat is usually used for this type of sausage. After they have been stuffed into casings, these sausages are smoked and cooked. These smoked sausages are fully cooked.

The last type of sausage is dry sausage. Besides chopped meat and spices, a curing agent such as salt or saltpeter is added to the initial sausage mixture. This meat mixture is then allowed to cure (or ferment) for several days, either before or after it is stuffed into casings. If

A variety of sausage links

Complementary sausage accompaniments → include cheese, potato salad, sauerkraut, pickled beets, cucumber pickles, and mustard.

Sausage Chart		
Name	Description	Serving Suggestions
Berliner	A cooked, smoked sausage made of cured pork and usually some beef. Keep refrigerated.	Serve cold with beer and rye bread.
Blood sausage	Cooked sausage of pork, seasonings, and beef blood. Refrigerate.	Serve in sandwiches or on cold plates.
Bockwurst	Fresh sausage made of ground pork, veal, eggs, and spices. Keep refrigerated; use promptly.	Simmer, then fry. Serve with sauerkraut, cabbage, or beans.
Bologna	Mild, smoked and cooked, beef and pork sausage. Sold in rings, sticks, and slices. Refrigerate.	Serve cold with cheese or in sandwiches.
Bratwurst	Made of pork and beef or pork and veal, and spices. Keep refrigerated; use promptly.	Grill or simmer and fry.
Cappicola	A lightly smoked, dried pork sausage seasoned with paprika and red pepper. Keep refrigerated.	Serve in sandwiches or on cold plates.
Cervelat	Smoked, dried sausage made of beef and pork. Keep refrigerated.	Serve on cold plates, in sandwiches, or creamed on toast.
Chorizos	Lightly smoked, dried pork sausage containing pimiento. Refrigerate.	Use in soups and in vegetable combinations.
Cotto salami	Pork and beef sausage seasoned with garlic and whole peppercorns. Keep refrigerated.	Use on pizza, in other Italian dishes, or serve cold in salads.
Frankfurters	Ground pork and beef. Fully cooked and smoked during manufacture. Keep refrigerated.	Use in buns, with sauerkraut, or in casseroles.
Fresh pork sausage	Ground pork seasoned with spices. Sold in bulk, patties, or links. Keep refrigerated; use promptly.	As an accompaniment for eggs or pancakes and in casseroles.
Frizzes	All-pork sausage sold in two types—with sweet spices and with hot spices. Refrigerate.	Good sandwich meat. Also serve in Italian dishes.
Genoa salami	All-pork dry sausage seasoned with garlic and sometimes wine. Keep refrigerated.	Use in sandwiches or in Italian dishes.

Sausage Chart		
Name	Description	Serving Suggestions
Italian pork sausage	Made of pork, and highly seasoned with garlic and other spices. Keep refrigerated; use promptly.	Use on pizza or in spaghetti sauce.
Italian salami	A pork and beef, dry sausage that is highly seasoned. Refrigerate.	Serve with dark bread or crackers as a snack.
Knackwurst	Similar to frankfurters in ingredients but seasoned with garlic. Keep refrigerated.	Serve with sauerkraut, with potato salad, and in casseroles.
Lebanon bologna	All-beef, cooked and smoked sausage. Keep refrigerated.	Serve on cold plates, in salads, or with sharp cheese.
Liver sausage	Made of pork and pork livers. Smooth texture; slices or spreads easily. Keep refrigerated.	Serve cold in sandwiches or on crackers.
Mortadella	Made of beef, pork, and fat; contains garlic. Refrigerate.	Use cold in sandwiches or heat and serve with a sauce.
Pastrami	Smoked, dried, beef sausage seasoned with garlic, cumin, and other spices. Refrigerate.	Serve hot or cold in sandwiches.
Pepperoni	Made of pork and sometimes beef, seasoned with pepper. Sold in large links. Keep refrigerated.	Slice thinly and use in Italian dishes, especially pizza.
Polish sausage	Cooked and smoked pork and beef sausage seasoned with garlic and coriander. Keep refrigerated.	Fry and serve for breakfast.
Smoked thuringer	A cooked and smoked, pork and beef sausage found primarily in the Midwest. Keep refrigerated.	Grill and serve in buns.
Summer sausage	Made of beef, beef heart, and pork. Mildly seasoned and dried. Keep refrigerated.	Serve as snack, in sandwiches, or cooked with cabbage.
Vienna sausage	Mild, tiny, canned sausage links that are lightly smoked.	Serve as a cocktail snack or in casseroles.
Weisswurst	A mildly seasoned, pork and veal sausage characterized by its light color. Keep refrigerated; use promptly.	Serve fried for breakfast.

the sausage is smoked, this is done after curing. The most important step in making dry sausage is the air-drying process. This is done under specially controlled conditions of humidity and other factors. Pepperoni, salami, pastrami, summer sausage, cappicola, and other types of dry sausage can be served cold or hot.

How to store: Sausages that belong to the first four types—fresh; uncooked, smoked; cooked; and cooked, smoked—require storage in the refrigerator. Like other fresh meat, fresh sausage is highly perishable, so use it a day or two after purchase. Sausages that have been cooked and/or smoked can be kept longer.

Although uncut dry sausages will keep in any cool, dry storage place, refrigeration is recommended for long periods of storage. After the sausage is cut, it definitely needs to be refrigerated.

Because freezing affects the flavor of the fat in sausage, freezer storage is not recommended for sausages.

How to use: Italian sausage pizza, sausage patties and scrambled eggs, frankfurters in buns, sausage casseroles, apples and sausage links, sausage and sauerkraut, bologna sandwiches, and salami and cheese are only a few examples of popular uses for sausage. Quite naturally, the wide selection of sausages that are available has led to the development of numerous uses for sausage. Not only is it easy to use your favorite kind of sausage in several different ways, but it is also easy to acquaint your family with a wide selection of sausages served in a variety of ways. (See also *Pork.*)

Snapperoni Franks

Cover 6 frankfurters with cold water; bring to boiling. Simmer 5 minutes. In saucepan slightly mash one 21-ounce can pork and beans in tomato sauce with a fork. Blend in ½ cup diced pepperoni, ¼ cup catsup, and 2 tablespoons sweet pickle relish. Cook and stir until mixture is heated through. Split and toast 6 frankfurter buns. Place franks in buns; spoon pepperoni-bean mixture over franks. Serves 6.

Easy Italian Chicken

    ¼ cup all-purpose flour
    ½ teaspoon paprika
    ½ teaspoon dried oregano leaves,
        crushed
    ¼ teaspoon garlic salt
    1 2½- to 3-pound ready-to-cook
        broiler-fryer chicken, cut up
    ½ pound link sausages, sliced
    1 16-ounce can tomatoes, cut up

Combine first 4 ingredients and 2 teaspoons salt; coat chicken pieces with flour mixture. Brown sausage in large, shallow baking pan at 400° about 15 minutes. Remove pan from oven; pour off excess fat. Stir in *half* of the tomatoes. Place chicken, skin side down, in a single layer in pan. Bake at 400° for 30 minutes. Turn the chicken. Add remaining tomatoes and bake until browned, 45 minutes longer. Spoon sauce over the chicken. Makes 4 servings.

Frank Triangles

    8 frankfurters
      Butter or margarine
    8 slices bread, crusts removed
    ¼ cup grated Parmesan cheese
    3 tablespoons prepared mustard
    3 tablespoons finely chopped onion
   16 pimiento-stuffed green olives

Place frankfurters in cold water; bring to boiling and simmer 5 minutes. Drain.

Butter one side of bread; dip buttered side in cheese. Spread other side with mustard. Sprinkle each mustard-spread side with about 1 teaspoon onion. Place a frank diagonally across each slice. Fasten two opposite corners of each slice, cheese side out, with wooden picks. Place on side on broiler rack. Broil 3 inches from heat 2 to 3 minutes. Turn triangles over. Broil 2 to 3 minutes more. Trim with olives on wooden picks. Makes 8 servings.

Hearty meal-on-a-platter

Fluffy whipped potatoes surround the other-foods—weinkraut, sausages, boiled beef, and pig's knuckles—that make up Hausplatte.

Individual Sausage and Muffin Bake casseroles combine English muffins, a sausage mixture, and tomato (see *Pork* for recipe).

Sausage in Biscuits

Convenience foods give you a head start—

> 1 8-ounce package refrigerated biscuits (10)
> **Prepared mustard**
> 1 4-ounce can Vienna sausages
> • • •
> 1 10-ounce package frozen peas in cream sauce

Pat out *seven* biscuits lengthwise*; spread lightly with mustard. Roll each Vienna sausage in a biscuit; seal edges with fingers. Place biscuits, seam side down, on small baking sheet; bake at 425° for about 10 minutes.

Prepare frozen peas in cream sauce following package directions. Spoon the cooked peas over the biscuits. Makes 7 sausage rolls.

*If desired, bake remaining biscuits.

Sausage Kabobs

Alternate brown-and-serve sausages, canned peach halves with a maraschino cherry in center, and mushroom caps on skewers. Brush generously with melted butter. Broil the kabobs 4 to 5 inches from coals till heated through, about 5 minutes on each side.

Hausplatte

> **Precooked bratwurst**
> **Knackwurst**
> **Duchess Potatoes**
> **Weinkraut**
> **Corned Pig's Knuckles**
> **Boiled Beef**
> **Mustard**
> **Horseradish**

Grill bratwurst and heat knackwurst briefly in boiling water. On a large, oval, seasoned plank, make a border with Duchess Potatoes. Fill center with Weinkraut. Top with these: Corned Pig's Knuckles, Boiled Beef, grilled bratwurst, and cooked knackwurst. Baste the meats with Burgundy gravy from Boiled Beef. Broil 5 to 8 minutes to brown the potatoes lightly. Pass mustard and horseradish.

Duchess Potatoes: Combine 4 cups hot mashed potatoes, 1 tablespoon butter, and 2 beaten egg yolks; season with salt and pepper. Mix well. Using No. 7 or No. 9 star tip, pipe the hot mixture around the rim of the plank; drizzle with 2 tablespoons melted butter.

Corned Pig's Knuckles: In saucepan cover corned pig's knuckles with fresh water. Add 1 small onion, halved, a few peppercorns, and a few bay leaves. Simmer till tender, about 2½ to 3 hours; remove meat from water.

Weinkraut: Finely chop 1 small onion; cook in ¼ cup butter or margarine till onion is just tender. Add 2 tablespoons brown sugar and let melt. Add ½ teaspoon salt; 1 teaspoon vinegar; 1½ cups dry white wine; 1 cup chicken broth; 1 small potato, grated; and 4 cups sauerkraut, drained. Cook, uncovered, for 30 minutes. Add 2 green apples, peeled and diced, and the cooked Corned Pig's Knuckles. Cover and simmer 30 minutes more. Drain the sauerkraut and remove the Pig's Knuckles.

Boiled Beef: Rub 4 pounds fresh lean beef short ribs with 1½ teaspoons salt; place in pot and cover with boiling water. Bring quickly back to boil; cook 10 minutes. Skim top.

Add 2 or 3 sprigs parsley; 4 peppercorns; and ½ teaspoon dried thyme leaves, crushed. Cover; cook slowly 3 hours. Last half hour add 2 onions, 2 carrots, 1 parsnip, 1 turnip, and 1 bay leaf. Lift out chunks of meat. Boil stock until reduced to rich gravy. Add about ¼ cup Burgundy to ¾ cup stock. Spoon some gravy over meats before broiling. Pass remainder.

Bologna Baskets

    6 or 8 slices bologna
    2 tablespoons shortening
    1 16-ounce can German-style
       potato salad
    Paprika

In stacks of 2 slices each, heat bologna in hot shortening in skillet until meat forms cups. Heat potato salad. Fill bologna cups with potato salad. Sprinkle with paprika. Serve individually or as a garnish. Serves 3 or 4.

SAUTÉ *(sō tā′, sô-)* — To cook quickly in a very small amount of fat. Since sautéing is done rapidly, the food cooked in this way must be thin in order to cook thoroughly. Vegetables such as onions are often sautéed before using them.

SAUTERNE, SAUTERNES *(sō tûrń, sô-)* — 1. A very rich and sweet, golden-hued wine that is made in the Sauternes region of France. In this context, the name of the wine is properly spelled sauternes. **2.** The generic name for a category of dry to sweet white wines that are produced in the United States. The final s is left off when denoting a United States wine.

Sauternes of France: Five townships in southern France legally comprise the area in which French sauternes are made. Even though a wine producer just outside this region produces wine from the same type of grapes and in the same manner, he cannot call it wine sauterne.

According to legend, the first French sauternes was developed accidentally at the Yquem château. Reportedly, the grapes at that château reached the peak of their maturity while the owner was away. When he returned, the grapes were overmature, shriveled, and covered with a mold. The owner harvested the grapes anyway and processed them into wine. What resulted was a uniquely rich, sweet wine that is now known as sauternes.

Today, scientists understand what changes the grapes undergo during the ripening. As the three varieties grown in this region—Semillon, Sauvignon blanc, and Muscadelle—pass their peak of ripeness, the sun causes the grapes to shrivel and dehydrate. This increases the concentration of sugar in the grapes. At the same time, a specific mold, *Botrytis cinerea*, which gives the wine its unusual and characteristic aroma, develops on and penetrates through the fruit skins. These changes are called the noble rot.

The high sugar content and the yeast produced by noble rot are a hindrance in making dry wine, but they are essential if a natural sweet wine is desired. To make sauternes, therefore, harvesting the grapes just at this noble rot stage is of utmost importance. Oftentimes, the grapes must be picked one by one in a series of harvests. The grapes are picked only when the sun is high in the sky so that any dew on the grapes has evaporated. Fermentation and bottling of sauternes are similar to other wines.

Uses of French sauternes: Because of the intense sweetness, sauternes is categorized as a dessert wine. When used as a dessert beverage, it should be served at cool room temperature, 60° to 70°. Sauternes is also used as an ingredient in desserts, particularly fruit-flavored ones.

Sauterne of the United States: A wine designated as sauterne (without the s) by a United States winery has quite different specifications than those of a French sauternes. Although golden in color, these sauternes are, in general, dry to semisweet table wines. There are a few sweet, American-produced sauternes.

Unlike French sauternes, there are no set grape varieties that must be used in the production of a United States sauterne. Any variety that produces a wine within the American defined limits of the sauterne category can be used. Some of the better United States-produced sauternes are made from one or more of the traditional varieties. Under federal law, if the wine contains over 51 percent of this varietal grape, it may be given that varietal name, such as Semillon.

Three names—dry sauterne, sauterne, and sweet, haut, or château sauterne—are applied to United States-produced

wines to indicate the relative dryness or sweetness of the wines. What determines the name used on the sauterne label is not legally defined in this country. Instead, each vintner determines his own specifications for the three types.

Sauterne as produced in the United States parallels that of other wines. Harvesting is carried out in one session. A very few premium sauternes are produced from grapes to which *Botrytis cinerea* usually must be induced artificially. These wines, quite naturally, command higher prices at the stores.

Uses of United States-produced sauterne: In order to determine how to use a sauterne that has been produced in the United States, it is essential that you know whether the wine is dry or sweet.

The drier sauterne types are used as entree accompaniments or ingredients. Poultry, fish, shellfish, veal, and cheese complement the delicate flavor of sauterne. When served as the beverage of the meal, the wine should be 45° to 50°.

Sweeter sauternes should be used in a dessert fashion as are the French sauternes. (See also *Wines and Spirits*.)

Sauterne Sauce

¼ cup dry sauterne
1 tablespoon instant minced onion

• • •

¾ cup mayonnaise or salad
   dressing
2 tablespoons snipped parsley
1 tablespoon lemon juice

In small saucepan combine sauterne and instant minced onion; let stand about 10 minutes. Add mayonnaise or salad dressing, snipped parsley, and lemon juice. Heat, stirring constantly, over low heat. Makes 1 cup sauce.

Dessert elegance

← Decoratively mound sweetened whipped cream in the center of the cake as the finishing touch to delicious Savarin Chantilly.

Wine-Broiled Chicken

Combine ¼ cup dry sauterne; ¼ cup salad oil; ¼ cup chopped onion; 2 teaspoons bottled steak sauce; 2 teaspoons lemon juice; 1 teaspoon dry mustard; 1 teaspoon salt; ⅛ teaspoon dried thyme leaves, crushed; ⅛ teaspoon dried marjoram leaves, crushed; ⅛ teaspoon dried rosemary leaves, crushed; and dash pepper. Mix well; cover and let stand several hours at room temperature or overnight in refrigerator to blend flavors.

Brush two 2- to 2½-pound ready-to-cook broiler-fryer chickens, split in halves lengthwise or in quarters, with wine mixture. Place, skin side down, in broiler pan (without rack). Broil the chicken 5 to 7 inches from heat till lightly browned, about 20 minutes. Brush occasionally with the wine mixture. Turn; broil till done, about 15 to 20 minutes longer, brushing occasionally with mixture. Serves 4.

Herbed Chicken Bake

A company special main dish—

Prepare one 6-ounce package long-grain, wild rice mix according to package directions. Bone 3 large chicken breasts; halve lengthwise. Season with salt and pepper.

In skillet slowly brown boned chicken in ¼ cup butter or margarine. Spoon cooked rice into 1½-quart casserole; top with chicken pieces, skin side up. Add one 10½-ounce can condensed cream of chicken soup to skillet; slowly add ¾ cup dry sauterne, stirring till smooth. Stir in ½ cup sliced celery; one 3-ounce can sliced mushrooms, drained; and 2 tablespoons chopped, canned pimiento. Bring soup mixture to boil; pour over chicken. Cover; bake at 350° for 25 minutes. Uncover; bake till chicken is tender, 20 minutes. Serves 6.

SAVARIN *(sav'uh rin)*—A rich, yeast cake baked in a ring mold, then steeped in a sugar syrup flavored with rum, another liquor, or fruit juice. A savarin is often glazed, decorated, and served with whipped cream. The mold in which this cake is baked is also called a savarin.

A baba is similar to a savarin, but it is traditionally baked in a flared mold.

Savarin Chantilly

    1 package active dry yeast
    2 cups sifted all-purpose flour
    ¾ cup milk
    6 tablespoons butter or margarine
    ¼ cup sugar
    1 egg
      Savarin Syrup
      Apricot Glaze
      Blanched almonds
      Candied cherries
      Creme Chantilly

In large mixer bowl combine yeast and *1½ cups* flour. Heat milk, butter or margarine, sugar, and ½ teaspoon salt just till warm, stirring occasionally to melt butter. Add to dry mixture in mixer bowl; add egg. Beat at low speed of electric mixer for ½ minute, scraping sides of bowl constantly. Beat 3 minutes at high speed. By hand stir in remaining flour.

Cover; let rise in warm place till double, about 1¼ hours. Stir down batter; spoon into a well-greased 6½-cup ring mold. Cover; let rise till almost double, about 45 minutes.

Bake at 350° till top is browned, about 35 minutes. Cool 5 minutes, then remove from mold; place on rack on baking sheet. With a meat fork, prick top of ring in several places. Gradually drizzle Savarin Syrup, a small amount at a time, over ring, till all syrup is absorbed. Let stand about 30 minutes. Then, drizzle on Apricot Glaze. Trim top with blanched almonds and candied cherries. At serving time, fill center with Creme Chantilly. Serves 14.

Savarin Syrup: Combine ¾ cup sugar and 1½ cups water; bring to boil. Cool to lukewarm. Stir in ½ cup cognac, rum, *or* kirsch.

Apricot Glaze: In small saucepan cook and stir one 12-ounce jar apricot preserves (about 1¼ cups) over low heat till melted; sieve.

Creme Chantilly: In mixing bowl whip 2 cups whipping cream with 2 tablespoons confectioners' sugar and 2 teaspoons vanilla.

SAVORY *(sā′vuh rē)* – **1.** An herb belonging to the mint family. **2.** A nonsweet tidbit served in England at the end of a meal. These savories resemble appetizers, but instead of being served at the beginning of the meal, they are served after the dessert to clear the palate.

Savory, the herb, is a native of southern Europe where it is not only used as a seasoning but also as pillow stuffing because of its pleasing fragrance.

This herb is well known in two varieties. Winter savory is a perennial bushy herb; summer savory is a somewhat-scraggly annual plant. Both varieties can be quite easily grown in herb gardens, but the dried savory available in supermarkets is the milder summer savory.

The flavor of savory leaves is aromatic and slightly resinous. This is an herb that seems purposely made for all kinds of fresh beans. In fact, its German name means bean herb. However, savory also adds a pleasingly distinctive flavor to tossed salads, sauerkraut, cabbage, peas, scrambled eggs, fish, many sauces, and poultry dishes. Savory is frequently used in stuffings, and it is an ingredient in most poultry seasoning mixtures. As with other seasonings, use only enough savory to season the food. (See also *Herb*.)

Savory Green Beans

    2 16-ounce cans green beans
    3 tablespoons butter or margarine,
      melted
    2 tablespoons chopped canned
      pimiento
    1 teaspoon dried savory leaves,
      crushed
    ¼ teaspoon salt
      Dash pepper

Heat beans in their liquid; drain well. Return beans to pan. Combine butter, pimiento, savory, salt, and pepper; pour over beans. Toss lightly to coat. Makes 8 servings.

SAVOY CABBAGE – A green cabbage variety, named for the Savoy region in France, that has large, curly and wrinkled leaves that form into a moderately loose head. The shape of the leaves makes them especially good for the wrappers of stuffed cabbage rolls. (See also *Cabbage*.)

SCALD – To heat a liquid to a temperature just below the boiling point.

SCALE – **1.** A flat, hard plate that makes up the covering on fish. **2.** To remove this covering from a fish. **3.** A piece of equipment used for weighing foods.

To scale a fish, first wash it thoroughly. Fish are easier to scale when wet, so do not dry. If the fish was washed earlier, dip it in cold water for a few minutes. Then, place on a flat surface and scrape the scales off with a knife or scraper. Hold the instrument almost vertically, and move from the tail toward the head.

The piece of household equipment known as a scale comes in several types. One has a sliding weight like a doctor's scales. Another has a spring balance.

A scale in the home can improve accuracy in measuring and save time. Use the scale to weigh meats, vegetables, and cheeses. If these foods are placed in a dish or pan before weighing, be sure to subtract the extra weight of the container.

It's easy to halve mixtures accurately and quickly if you first weigh the total amount and then remove part of the mixture until the scale registers half of the original weight. This comes in handy when dividing cookie doughs, cake batters, candies, candied fruits, and sauces.

Follow the instruction booklet for correct use and care of equipment. Check the scale occasionally with weights, if possible, to see that it is accurate.

SCALLION *(skal' yuhn)* – Another name for the immature-bulbed green onion. There is some possibility that the name, scallion, was derived from the Palestinian seaport of Ascalon. (See also *Green Onion.*)

SCALLOP – A shellfish in a saucer-shaped, two-part shell. Except that scallops are more active, they are similar to oysters and clams. Their large muscle, sometimes called the eye, opens and closes the shell to propel them through water. This muscle, firm and delicately sweet, is the only part eaten by Americans, although Europeans eat the entire shellfish.

The nutritional value of scallops centers around their high-quality protein. The meat also contains minerals and fat. A 3½-ounce serving, steamed, has 110 calories; breaded and fried, 195 calories.

The principal types of scallops are bay, sea, and calico. Bay scallops live inshore along the New England and Gulf coasts. They are small and have a grooved or ridged shell. The creamy pink, tan, or white meat has a more tender texture and more delicate flavor than the sea scallop.

Sea scallops live along the north and middle parts of the Atlantic coast. They are larger and whiter than those from the bay, and their shells are not ridged.

Calico scallops closely resemble bay scallops. They were discovered recently along the Florida and North Carolina coasts. Calicos are expected to be available to the consumer in the future.

The boats that catch scallops also dress and pack them at sea. The shells are opened and the muscles removed. These muscles are marketed fresh or frozen. Frozen ones are cooked or breaded.

When purchasing fresh scallops, look for those with little or no liquid and a sweet odor. Keep chilled and use promptly.

Eat scallops raw like oysters and clams, or bake, broil, fry, or boil them before eating. Dishes made with scallops are served as entrées, appetizers, and salads. Use either fresh or frozen scallops in recipes; frozen ones are usually thawed before cooking. Allow ½ to ⅓ pound for each serving. (See also *Shellfish.*)

Deep-Fried Scallops

Drain scallops; dry between paper toweling. Roll in all-purpose flour seasoned with salt and pepper. Dip into mixture of 1 beaten egg and 1 tablespoon water, then fine dry bread crumbs. Fry in deep, hot fat (375°) till golden, about 2 minutes. Drain on paper toweling. Serve scallops hot; pass tartar sauce.

Broiled Scallops

Use 2 pounds fresh or frozen scallops. Thaw frozen scallops. Place in shallow baking pan. Sprinkle with salt, pepper, and paprika. Dot with butter. Broil 3 inches from heat till lightly browned, about 6 to 9 minutes. Serve with lemon wedges or tartar sauce and garnish with parsley, if desired. Serves 6.

Hot Scallop Chowder

1 pound fresh or frozen scallops
2 cups boiling water
1 teaspoon salt

• • •

1 10½-ounce can condensed cream
    of chicken soup
1 10½-ounce can condensed cream
    of potato soup
1½ cups milk
1 cup light cream
2 teaspoons snipped chives

Thaw frozen scallops. Rinse and chop coarsely. Place in boiling, salted water. Return to boil. Reduce heat; simmer 1 minute. Drain. Combine soups and milk in blender container or mixer bowl. Blend or beat till smooth. Pour into saucepan; stir in cream and chives. Heat just to boiling, stirring occasionally. Add scallops; heat through. Pour into soup bowls; top with snipped chives, if desired. Serves 6.

Scallops Mornay

An elegant casserole—

Combine ½ cup dry sauterne, ¾ cup water, ¼ teaspoon salt, ¼ teaspoon instant minced onion, and dash pepper in saucepan. Simmer 5 minutes. Add 8 ounces frozen scallops (halve or quarter if large) and ½ cup sliced fresh mushrooms. Cover and simmer 5 minutes. Remove scallops and mushrooms; set aside.

Cook stock in saucepan till reduced to ½ cup, about 15 minutes. Melt 1 tablespoon butter or margarine in another saucepan; stir in 1½ tablespoons all-purpose flour. Stir in fish stock and ½ cup milk; cook and stir till mixture thickens and bubbles. Add ¼ cup grated process Swiss cheese, stirring till melted. Season with salt and pepper, if desired.

Remove from heat; add scallops and mushrooms. Spoon into two individual baking dishes. Bake at 375° for 15 to 20 minutes. Trim with 1 to 2 tablespoons snipped parsley. Serves 2.

For an easy-to-prepare main dish, try Corn and Chicken Scallop. Place chicken drumsticks atop the corn and onion mixture and bake. Mushrooms and parsley, added later, complete the dish.

Scallops Tetrazzini

Thaw one 12-ounce package frozen scallops; cut scallops in halves. In saucepan combine scallops, ½ teaspoon instant minced onion, ¼ teaspoon salt, and dash pepper. Add 1 cup water. Cover; simmer 10 minutes. Drain; reserve ½ cup cooking liquid. Melt 2 tablespoons butter. Blend in 2 tablespoons all-purpose flour; ½ teaspoon paprika; 1 drop bottled hot pepper sauce; dash dried oregano leaves, crushed; and dash salt. Add the ½ cup cooking liquid and ½ cup milk. Cook and stir till thickened. Stir a little hot mixture into 1 slightly beaten egg. Return to sauce; mix well.

Add one 3-ounce can broiled, sliced mushrooms with liquid and scallops to sauce. Mix well. Spoon 4 ounces spaghetti, cooked and drained, into a 10x6x1¾-inch baking dish. Top the spaghetti with the scallop mixture; sprinkle with 2 tablespoons grated Parmesan cheese. Broil about 5 minutes. Makes 4 servings.

Scallops and Bacon

1 pound fresh or frozen scallops

• • •

¼ cup butter or margarine, melted
2 tablespoons lemon juice
½ teaspoon salt
Dash white pepper

• • •

Sliced bacon
Paprika

Thaw frozen scallops. Remove any shell particles and wash. Combine butter or margarine, lemon juice, salt, and pepper. Pour mixture over scallops; let stand for 30 minutes, turning once. Drain the scallops.

Cut bacon slices in half lengthwise. In a skillet partially cook bacon until it begins to ruffle, but is still flexible. Drain on paper toweling and let cool.

Wrap each of the scallops with a piece of partially cooked bacon and hold the bacon in place with a wooden pick. Place the bacon-wrapped scallops in a wire broiler basket. Sprinkle topside with paprika.

Broil over *medium-hot* coals for 5 minutes. Turn and sprinkle with paprika. Broil second side of scallops until bacon is crisp and brown, about 5 to 7 minutes. Serve while hot.

Scallop Salad

Thaw 1½ pounds frozen scallops. Place scallops and 2 tablespoons salt in 1 quart boiling water. Cover; return to boiling. Reduce heat; simmer 3 to 4 minutes. Drain and cool; slice. Combine cooked scallops; one 10-ounce package frozen green beans, cooked and drained; 1 cup sliced celery; 2 tablespoons chopped green onion; 2 tablespoons chopped green pepper; and 2 tablespoons chopped, canned pimiento.

In screw-top jar combine ½ cup vinegar; 1 tablespoon salad oil; 1 tablespoon sugar; ¼ teaspoon salt; ¼ teaspoon dried tarragon leaves, crushed; and dash pepper. Cover and shake. Pour vinegar mixture over scallop mixture. Cover; chill at least 1 hour, stirring occasionally. Drain before serving. Spoon salad into lettuce cups. Makes 6 servings.

Scallops Elegant

1 pound fresh or frozen scallops
½ cup finely chopped celery
¼ cup chopped onion
1 small clove garlic, minced
3 tablespoons butter or margarine
¼ cup fine saltine cracker crumbs
1 tablespoon snipped parsley
1 tablespoon all-purpose flour
¼ teaspoon paprika
½ cup milk
2 tablespoons dry sherry
¼ cup shredded process Swiss cheese

Cook scallops; cut large scallops in half. Cook celery, onion, and garlic in *2 tablespoons* butter till tender but not brown. Stir in scallops, crumbs, and parsley. Turn into an 8-inch pie plate. Melt remaining butter. Blend in flour, paprika, and ⅛ teaspoon salt. Add milk all at once. Cook and stir till thickened and bubbly. Remove from heat; stir in sherry. Pour sauce over scallops; sprinkle cheese atop. Bake at 425° for 15 minutes. Serves 4.

SCALLOPED—Foods combined with a saucy mixture that often contains cracker or bread crumbs, then baked. Scalloped vegetables, poultry, and seafood are excellent dishes to prepare several hours ahead and keep refrigerated.

Delectable Scalloped Corn and Oysters makes a perfect vegetable accompaniment for meat dishes such as roast turkey.

Corn and Chicken Scallop

Meat and vegetable cook in one dish—

>   1 17-ounce can cream-style corn
>   1 cup milk
>   1 egg
>   1 tablespoon all-purpose flour
>   6 green onions and tops, snipped
>   6 to 8 chicken drumsticks
>   Paprika
>   Seasoned salt
>   30 saltine crackers
>   1/4 cup butter or margarine
>   1 3-ounce can sliced mushrooms,
>   drained

In a large, shallow casserole (or 13x9x2-inch baking dish), thoroughly combine cream-style corn, milk, egg, flour, and snipped onions. Generously sprinkle drumsticks with paprika; arrange over corn. Dash with seasoned salt. Crumble crackers over all. Dot with chunks of butter. Bake at 350° till chicken is tender, about 1 hour. Place mushrooms in center of casserole. Return to oven to heat. Garnish with parsley, if desired. Serves 3 or 4.

Scalloped Corn Supreme

>   1 17-ounce can cream-style corn
>   1 cup milk
>   1 well-beaten egg
>   1 cup saltine cracker crumbs
>   1/4 cup finely chopped onion
>   3 tablespoons chopped, canned
>   pimiento
>   3/4 teaspoon salt
>   1/2 cup buttered cracker crumbs

Heat corn and milk. Gradually stir in egg. Add next 4 ingredients and dash pepper. Mix well. Pour into greased 8-inch round baking dish. Top with buttered crumbs. Bake at 350° for 20 minutes. Makes 6 servings.

Scalloped Corn and Oysters

Combine one 17-ounce can cream-style corn; one 10½-ounce can frozen condensed oyster stew, thawed (if desired, reserve a few of the oysters from stew for garnish); 1 cup medium saltine cracker crumbs; 1 cup milk; ¼ cup finely chopped celery; 1 slightly beaten egg; 1 tablespoon finely chopped, canned pimiento; ¼ teaspoon salt, and dash pepper. Pour into greased 1½-quart casserole. Combine 2 tablespoons butter, melted, and ½ cup saltine cracker crumbs. Sprinkle over corn mixture in wreath design. Bake at 350° for 45 minutes. Garnish with reserved oysters; bake till knife inserted halfway between center and edge comes out clean, 15 minutes. Serves 6.

Scalloped Potatoes

In saucepan melt 3 tablespoons butter or margarine over low heat. Blend in 2 tablespoons all-purpose flour, 1½ teaspoons salt, and ⅛ teaspoon pepper. Add 3 cups milk all at once. Cook quickly, stirring till thickened and bubbly. Remove mixture from heat.*

Peel and thinly slice 6 medium potatoes (6 cups). Place *half* the potatoes in greased 2-quart casserole; cover with 1 tablespoon chopped onion and *half* the sauce. Repeat layers, using another tablespoon chopped onion. Cover and bake at 350° about 1 hour. Uncover; bake 30 minutes. Serves 4 to 6.

*Shredded cheese may be added to sauce.

Scalloped Bacon and Eggs

- ¼ cup chopped onion
- 2 tablespoons butter or margarine
- 2 tablespoons all-purpose flour
- 1½ cups milk
- 4 ounces sharp process American cheese, shredded (1 cup)
- 6 hard-cooked eggs, sliced
- 1½ cups crushed potato chips
- 10 to 12 slices bacon, crisp-cooked and crumbled

Cook onion in butter till tender, but not brown; blend in flour. Add milk. Cook, stirring constantly, till mixture is thickened and bubbly. Add cheese; stir till melted.

Place a layer of egg slices in 10x6x1½-inch baking dish. Cover with *half* the cheese sauce, *half* the potato chips, and *half* the bacon. Repeat layers. Bake at 350° for 15 to 20 minutes or till heated through. Serves 4.

Scalloped Squash

- 1 pound unpeeled, sliced summer squash (3 cups)
- 1 medium onion, cut in wedges
- 3 tablespoons butter or margarine
- 3 tablespoons all-purpose flour
- 1¼ cups milk
- 2 ounces process Swiss cheese, shredded (½ cup)

Cook squash and onion in boiling, salted water till tender, 10 minutes; drain. In saucepan melt butter; stir in flour, ½ teaspoon salt, and dash pepper. Add milk. Cook and stir till thick and bubbly. Add cheese; stir till melted. Add vegetables. Pour into 1½-quart casserole. Bake, uncovered, at 350° for 30 minutes. Serves 6.

SCALLOPINE, SCALLOPINI (*skä′ luh pē′ nē, skal′ uh*)—An Italian dish that contains thin, boneless pieces of meat, most commonly veal, called scallopine. The thin veal pieces sometimes are pounded even thinner before they are browned and cooked in a sauce, usually containing wine or tomatoes. In the United States, veal steaks or cutlets are used in recipes calling for the scallopine cut.

Veal Scallopine with Wine

- 1½ pounds veal cutlets, cut ¼ inch thick
- ⅓ cup all-purpose flour
- ¼ cup butter or margarine
- 1 tablespoon lemon juice
- 1 chicken bouillon cube
- ¼ cup dry white wine
- 1 3-ounce can sliced mushrooms, drained
- 2 tablespoons sliced ripe olives
- 2 tablespoons snipped parsley

Coat veal cutlets with flour. In large skillet, brown cutlets in hot butter or margarine, a few at a time. Place all browned cutlets in skillet. Add ½ cup water, lemon juice, chicken bouillon cube, and ⅛ teaspoon pepper. Simmer, covered, till tender, about 30 minutes. Remove cutlets to warm platter. Add dry white wine, drained mushrooms, sliced ripe olives, and snipped parsley to skillet. Heat just to boiling. Pour sauce over cutlets. Serves 6.

SCAMORZE (*ska môrd′ dzē*)—A fairly mild, yellowish white, Italian fresh cheese originally made of buffalo's milk but now often made of cow's or goat's milk. Scamorze is similar in flavor and appearance to another Italian cheese Mozzarella.

The manufacture of scamorze involves one unusual step—stretching the cheese until it is elastic. Afterward, it is molded into an oval the size of a large lemon, soaked in brine, and finally air dried.

In Italy, scamorze is particularly popular when toasted or fried and served with toast or fried eggs. (See also *Cheese.*)

SCAMPI (*skam′ pē*)—The Italian name of a shellfish of the Adriatic sea that is closely related to shrimp and prawns. The name is often mistakenly used to refer to any large variety of shrimp. It is also misused in the name of various shrimp dishes. On restaurant menus, although the listing "shrimp scampi" is redundant, it is understood to mean shrimp cooked in the Italian-style for scampi, that is, by broiling the whole shrimp including the tail and serving it with a sauce containing garlic and frequently olive oil.

SCANDINAVIAN COOKERY

*A look at the foods and food preparation
of Denmark, Sweden, Norway, and Finland.*

The great peninsula that extends from above the Arctic Circle to the North and Baltic seas encompasses three of the four countries that make up Scandinavia—Sweden, Finland, and Norway. The fourth country—Denmark—juts out from the European continent. Geography accounts for both similarities and differences in the basic foods of the four countries. For example, all of these countries have extensive seacoasts, and, as would be expected, fish and shellfish play an important part in the diet. However, mountainous Norway has little land available for growing food, while Sweden and Denmark have a long history of agricultural abundance. Finland, a land of lakes and forests, has a plentiful supply of game and wild foods, but little agricultural production.

The Scandinavians always have used a lot of seafood, particularly herring, which is still one of the most common dishes. Foods from the forests are also popular. This pattern has existed from the time of the Vikings, those hardy warlike people who roamed Scandinavia from the eighth to the tenth century. They gathered berries and nuts and hunted for elk and deer in the forests, and fished for herring, oysters, and mussels in the sea and inland fjords and lakes. Besides relying to a great extent on hunting and fishing for food,

the Vikings also raised chickens and geese and, at least to some extent, cultivated vegetables such as onions and cabbage.

From the Viking period through the successive years that resulted in the gradual development of four independent countries, all of Scandinavia was at some time a part of Sweden. The result is a thread of similarity that runs through the basic cuisine of the Scandinavian countries. This is particularly noticeable when you compare the foods of Denmark, Sweden, and Norway. Although the Swedish influence on the food pattern of Finland is still evident, it is somewhat overshadowed by the strong Russian influence that resulted from Finland's role as part of the Russian Empire for about 100 years—from the early 1800s to 1917.

Fish

Since all the Scandinavian countries have seacoast as part of their border, quite naturally the Scandinavians make use of the fish and seafood easily available. Fish is especially important in Norway and Finland, where little land is available for agricultural production. In fact, fish of one type or another is often eaten as many as six times a week. Because of this, you might assume that the Norwegians and Finns have a large collection of special fish recipes. But, this is not the case, since Norwegian and Finnish cooks generally use simple preparation methods such as grilling, steaming, and poaching.

This lack of fish recipes does not reflect on the imaginativeness of the natives at all. Rather it is proof that these people are

Scandinavian fare

← A Decorated Ham, Stuffed Celery, Quick Swedish Meatballs, and Swedish Brown Beans are part of a Swedish smorgasbord.

convinced that the best flavor fish can have is a fresh flavor. Since many kinds of fish are continually available, this fresh flavor is easily captured by serving fish that were caught only a few hours earlier.

The two fish that rank highest in importance in the Scandinavian countries are cod and herring. Even though these two fish have been abundant in Scandinavian waters for centuries, they never would have become a staple food and important export if the Scandinavians hadn't learned long ago how to preserve them.

Although some cod and herring are dried, pickled, or preserved in some other way, salting is the processing method most commonly used. When salting was first used, it was the only way the Scandinavians had of preserving their large catches. In fact, salted cod and herring kept so well that they could be shipped throughout Europe. They also became popular as food for lengthy journeys, particularly sea voyages. Today, however, more modern methods of preservation such as canning and freezing make salting no longer necessary as a preservative. Even so, the taste of salted fish is so appealing that thousands of salted cod and herring are produced each year for consumption in the Scandinavian countries as well as for shipment all over the world. In fact, almost all large United States supermarkets carry a selection of preserved fish products that are imported from the Scandinavian countries.

Besides salting, the Scandinavians have several distinctive ways of preserving and serving fish. For example, today's Norwegians retain an unusual fish dish from their ancestors, *lutefisk*. Codfish is soaked in a lye solution until it becomes a rather soft, somewhat jellylike mass. This is sometimes made at home, but more often bought ready to cook.

As with some dishes in the cuisine of almost any country, *lutefisk* is best-liked

Swedish bread

← Celebrate the holidays by serving festive Lucia Braid decorated with walnut halves and red and green candied cherries.

by people who acquired a taste for it during childhood and it is slow to gain favor with others. A second noteworthy Norwegian fish dish is fish pudding. This combination of fish, bread crumbs, and a thick sauce is served in most Norwegian homes about once a week.

Both the Swedes and the Norwegians continue to use age-old recipes to make fermented fish. The Swedes use herring to make their *surstromming*, while the Norwegians ferment trout. Although their preparation methods differ, both *surstromming* and fermented trout are potent concoctions that share with *lutefisk* the distinction of seeming peculiar to the majority of non-Scandinavians.

Lutefisk Special

Cook 8 small peeled potatoes in boiling, salted water till tender, about 25 to 35 minutes. Meanwhile, in saucepan bring 2 cups water and 1 teaspoon salt to boiling. Add 1 pound lutefisk, cut in serving-sized pieces. Cover and simmer till fish is tender, 15 minutes.

Melt 3 tablespoons butter or margarine in saucepan. Blend in 2 tablespoons all-purpose flour, ½ teaspoon salt, and ½ teaspoon dry mustard. Add 1¼ cups milk. Cook quickly, stirring constantly, till thickened and bubbly. Melt ½ cup butter or margarine. Serve mustard sauce over potatoes and melted butter or margarine with lutefisk. Makes 4 servings.

Horseradish-Sauced Steamed Fish

Use 1 pound fresh or frozen fish fillets or steaks, or one 3-pound dressed fish. Thaw frozen fish. Bring 2 cups water to boiling in 10-inch skillet or fish poacher with tight-fitting cover. Sprinkle fish with 1 teaspoon salt. Place fish on a greased rack in pan so that fish does not touch water. Cover pan tightly and steam till fish flakes easily when tested with a fork—fillets, 3 to 4 minutes; steaks, 6 to 8 minutes; dressed, 20 to 25 minutes. Carefully remove fish. Serve with chilled Horseradish Sauce.

Horseradish Sauce: In small mixing bowl combine 1 cup dairy sour cream, 3 tablespoons drained prepared horseradish, ¼ teaspoon salt, and dash paprika. Chill thoroughly.

Meat

Despite the abundance of fish that is available, Scandinavians also eat meats—pork, lamb, beef, poultry, and other meats. In fact, Denmark exports a large amount of pork and beef to the rest of Europe and to the British Isles.

In Denmark, pork is the favorite meat. Roasted pork, sometimes stuffed with fruit such as apples and figs, is one of the favorite pork dishes. However, it is by no means the only way pork is served. Pork chops, bacon, ham, pork loins, and other pork cuts are all used as main dishes. Pork pieces are used as stew meat or in casseroles, and ground pork is incorporated in casseroles and the popular meatballs or patties, called *frikadeller*.

Norway is a rugged mountainous land that will not support much domestic farming but is ideal for sheep raising. Norwegians seem to have inherited a love of mutton and wild game from their Viking ancestors. One Norwegian specialty is the dried, salted, and smoked leg of mutton, served in paper thin slices.

Beef, veal, pork, lamb, and poultry all have many uses in Swedish cookery. However, Swedish meatballs are probably the best-known Swedish meat dish. Characterized by their light texture which is achieved by adding mashed potatoes or milk-soaked bread to the meat mixture, these meatballs are a must at a smorgasbord and are also served at other meals.

Since much of Finland is covered with trees, the Finns have learned to appreciate the foods found in the deep forests. Game is plentiful and popular, and the Finnish cooks prepare it well. The Finns love of the wild taste is even carried to the cooking of domestic meats by using juniper berries to give forest flavor to poultry, or serving wild lingonberry preserves with many kinds of roasted meats.

Throughout Scandinavia, food is treated with respect, and thrift demands that none be wasted. To achieve this, the Scandinavians make many dishes that use variety meats. For example, a Danish meat dish called mock turtle is made from a calves head, and one of Finland's national favorites is a baked liver and rice dish.

Baked Liver and Rice (Finland)

An unusual, yet delicious casserole—

         2 cups water
         1 cup uncooked long-grain rice
         3 cups milk
       1/4 cup chopped onion
         1 tablespoon butter or margarine
    1 1/2 pounds beef liver, ground
           (2 1/2 cups)
       1/4 pound ground pork
       1/2 cup raisins
         3 tablespoons dark corn syrup
         2 teaspoons salt
    1 1/2 teaspoons dried marjoram leaves,
           crushed
           Dash pepper
           Canned cranberry sauce

In saucepan combine water and uncooked long-grain rice; bring to boiling, stirring once or twice. Simmer, uncovered, till water is absorbed, about 10 minutes. Add milk; cook over low heat, stirring occasionally, till the rice is tender, about 10 to 15 minutes. Meanwhile, cook chopped onion in butter or margarine till tender but not brown.

In mixing bowl combine cooked rice, cooked onion, ground liver, ground pork, raisins, dark corn syrup, salt, crushed marjoram, and pepper. Pour meat mixture into a well-greased 13x9x2-inch baking dish. Bake at 400° for 40 to 45 minutes. Serve hot accompanied by canned cranberry sauce. Makes 12 servings.

Glazed Yule Ham (Sweden)

    1 10- to 14-pound fully cooked
         ham
         Orange marmalade
    1 8-ounce package cream cheese,
         softened
         Cooked whole prunes (optional)
         Poached apple halves (optional)

Bake ham at 325° for 3 1/2 to 4 hours; 30 minutes before end of baking time, brush with orange marmalade. Cool ham. Put cream cheese into a pastry bag with a large decorator tip or into a syringe-type decorator. Press cheese out into desired piping atop ham. Garnish with prunes and apples, if desired.

Swedish Meatballs

¾ pound lean ground beef
½ pound ground veal
¼ pound ground pork
1½ cups soft bread crumbs
1 cup light cream
½ cup chopped onion
3 tablespoons butter or margarine
1 egg
¼ cup finely snipped parsley
1¼ teaspoons salt
Dash pepper
Dash ground ginger
Dash ground nutmeg
Gravy

Grind meats together twice. Soak bread in cream about 5 minutes. Cook onion in *1 tablespoon* of the butter till tender. Mix meats, crumb mixture, onion, egg, parsley, and seasonings. Beat 5 minutes at medium speed on electric mixer, or mix by hand till well combined. Chill. Shape into 1½-inch balls; brown in remaining butter. Remove from skillet. Make Gravy; add meat. Cover; cook 30 minutes, basting occasionally. Makes 30 meatballs.

Gravy: Melt 2 tablespoons butter in skillet with drippings. Stir in 2 tablespoons all-purpose flour. Add 1 beef bouillon cube dissolved in 1¼ cups boiling water and ½ teaspoon instant coffee powder. Cook, stirring constantly, till gravy is thickened and bubbly.

Serve guests a selection of Norwegian cookies and sweet breads including decoratively shaped Stag's Antlers, sugar dusted Fattigman (see *Fattigman* for recipe), and Cardamom Braid.

Baked goods and desserts

Scandinavian cooks are exceptionally fine bakers. Flavorful white bread, hearty rye bread, crisp cookies, flaky pastries, and many-layered cakes are all turned out in volume by the Scandinavians.

Two ingredients—cardamom and almonds—are used so extensively in Scandinavian baked goods that they are considered typically Scandinavian. The pleasant flavor of cardamom enhances cookies, cakes, and pastries. In fact, this spice is so popular that it often is sprinkled lightly on top of baked goods as well as being used in them. Almonds—sliced, chopped, ground, and in the form of almond paste—are widely used in Scandinavian cookies, cakes, sweet breads, and pastries.

Scandinavians traditionally keep more than one kind of cookie on hand to serve both invited and unexpected company. Since this requires frequent baking, the Scandinavians have become adept at making all kinds of cookies. Most of these cookies are characterized by a delightful crispness. Once this crispness was due to the use of salt of hartshorn as a leavening agent. Today, however, many Scandinavians use baking powder for leavening and rely on the buttery richness of the dough to produce the delicate crispness.

Borrow from Sweden and serve this delicious main dish, Swedish Meatballs. The gravy which accompanies the meatballs is subtly flavored with beef bouillon and instant coffee powder.

Although cooks from all four Scandinavian countries share the distinction of being good bakers, the baked goods they make differ from country to country. Denmark, Sweden, Norway, and Finland each have specialties of their own.

Danish baking is typified by the generous use of butter and cream. Fillings rich with cream are used between as many as six to eight layers of cake or pastry for elegant desserts, while butter adds richness to cakes, cookies, pastries, and many other delectable baked goods.

By far the best-known Danish specialty, and probably the best-known Scandinavian baked food, is Danish pastry. The rich, flaky breads and rolls that are known in other countries as typical Danish pastry are called *wienerbrod* (Vienna bread) or *dansk kage* (Danish cake) in Denmark. The popularity of Danish pastry is quickly apparent when you see the mammoth displays of pastries in shop windows along the streets of Danish cities. In fact, the Danes feel that a cup of coffee is lost without a Danish pastry, and so the hundreds of pastry shops ensure that there are enough of the pastries for everyone.

The multiple, flaky layers characteristic of Danish pastry are achieved by rolling butter into the yeast dough, folding, and then chilling the dough. From this basic dough, various pastries are made by varying the shape and/or filling.

Other Danish favorites include light textured *aebleskiver* (Danish doughnuts), baked in a special pan on top of the range, and the buttery, rich *sandkage*, which resembles an American pound cake.

The baking of Sweden, though not as rich in butter and cream as that of Denmark, is also delicious. Shades of color and flavor for rye bread loaves go from cakelike *limpa*, flavored with orange peel or caraway, to deep brown, hearty caraway rye. Sour milk bread that can be stacked in drawers is popular in northern Sweden. The thin, round rye disk with a hole in the middle is the flat bread preferred in the south. Swedish white flour baking centers on luscious coffee cakes and rolls with fruit or almond fillings, saffron and cardamom Christmas breads, thin and dainty pancakes (*plattar*), and waffles.

The Swedes also make dozens of types of cookies, some molded or cut into fancy shapes, some shaped with a cookie press, some sweet, and others richly spiced.

Norwegian cooks make especially good bread. Their sturdy rye bread loaves are round and slightly flattened. Flat bread is made of barley, rye, and oats, and buttered and sugared potato bread (*lefse*) is a holiday treat. However, Norwegians also turn out some fancier dishes. Their coffee cakes and tea rings are beautiful and delicious. Cookie baking keeps Norwegian cooks busy, especially before Christmas, turning out *kringle*, sand tarts (*sandbakkels*), and cardamom cookies.

Reflecting the characteristic heartiness of the typical Finnish diet, breads are especially important in Finland. Several grains (for example, wheat, oats, barley, and rye) are popularly used to make Finnish breads. Rye bread, ranging from moist, thick loaves to flat, hard loaves, is particularly favored. Other Finnish favorites, such as black bread and buckwheat pancakes, reflect the Russian influence on the Finnish cuisine.

Although sweet breads, cakes, and cookies often serve as dessert, the Scandinavians also enjoy other desserts, including puddings and fruit soups, although favorites vary from country to country.

The Danes are known for their love of food and to them, dessert is an essential part of the meal. Fresh fruits, puddings, fruit soups, and pancakes wrapped around a sweet filling all are enjoyed. And to perk up any dessert, the Danes just add some thick rich cream, often whipped.

In Norway, one of the national favorites is a hot sour cream porridge called *rommegrot*. This dessert is considered essential for holidays and other special occasions. Fruit soups and a red berry pudding called *rodgrot* are other Norwegian favorites.

In Sweden and Finland, berries are particularly plentiful and so are frequently used in desserts. Raspberries, strawberries, blueberries, and lingonberries are popularly used in puddings, tarts, and fruit soups. The Swedes especially enjoy thin pancakes filled or topped with lightly sweetened berries, and a special Finnish dessert is a whipped berry pudding.

Danish Pastry

Serve these extra-flaky pastries warm—

1½ cups butter
3½ to 4 cups sifted all-purpose
    flour
  2 packages active dry yeast
1¼ cups milk
¼ cup sugar
1 teaspoon salt
1 egg

    . . .

    Almond Filling
    Confectioners' Icing

Cream butter with ⅓ *cup* of the flour; pat or roll between 2 sheets of waxed paper to form a 12x6-inch rectangle. Chill thoroughly.

In large mixer bowl combine yeast and 1½ *cups* of the flour. Heat milk, sugar, and salt just till warm. Add to dry mixture in mixer bowl; add egg. Beat at low speed with electric mixer for ½ minute, scraping sides constantly. Beat 3 minutes at high speed. By hand, stir in enough remaining flour to make soft dough.

Turn out and knead on lightly floured surface until smooth and satiny, about 5 minutes. Let rest 10 minutes. Roll dough in a 14-inch square on lightly floured surface. Place the thoroughly chilled butter mixture on half the dough. Fold over other half of dough, pinching edges to seal. Roll dough on lightly floured surface into a 20x12-inch rectangle. Fold in thirds. (If butter softens, chill after each rolling.) Roll again into a 20x12-inch rectangle. Repeat the folding and rolling 2 more times. Chill at least 1 hour after last rolling.

Working on floured surface, shape dough into almond fans, twists, or bunting rolls. Place rolls on *ungreased* baking sheet. Let rise in warm place till almost double, 45 to 60 minutes. Bake at 425° for 8 to 10 minutes. If desired, brush tops immediately with Confectioners' Icing. Serve warm. Makes about 36.

Almond Filling: Thoroughly cream together ¼ cup butter or margarine and ¼ cup sugar. Add ¼ cup ground, blanched almonds and 1 to 2 drops almond flavoring; mix thoroughly.

Confectioners' Icing: Add sufficient light cream to 2 cups sifted confectioners' sugar to make of spreading consistency (about 2 tablespoons cream). Add 1 teaspoon vanilla and dash salt. Mix until smooth.

Shapes for Danish Pastry

Almond fans: Roll ⅓ of Danish Pastry dough into 12x9-inch rectangle. Cut in 4x2-inch pieces. Place 1 level teaspoon Almond Filling in center of each; fold lengthwise. Seal edges tightly; curve slightly. Snip side opposite sealed edge at 1-inch intervals.

Twists: Roll ⅓ of dough into 12x8-inch rectangle. Cut in 6x¾-inch strips. Hold ends of strip; twist in opposite directions. Form into circle, knot, figure-8, or snail shape.

Bunting rolls: Roll ⅓ of dough into 12x9-inch rectangle. Cut into 3-inch squares. Place 1 teaspoon Almond Filling in center of each. Fold opposite corners to center; overlap. Seal.

Cardamom Braid (Norway)

  1 package active dry yeast
2¾ to 3 cups sifted all-purpose
    flour
  ¾ teaspoon ground cardamom
  ¾ cup milk
  ¼ cup butter or margarine
  ⅓ cup sugar
  ½ teaspoon salt
  1 egg

In large mixer bowl combine yeast, ¾ *cup* of the flour, and cardamom. Heat together milk, butter or margarine, sugar, and salt till warm, stirring occasionally to melt butter. Add to dry mixture in mixer bowl; add egg. Beat at low speed with electric mixer for ½ minute, scraping sides of bowl constantly. Beat 3 minutes at high speed. By hand, stir in enough of the remaining flour to make a moderately soft dough. Turn out onto lightly floured surface; knead till smooth and elastic, 5 to 8 minutes. Place in lightly greased bowl, turning once to grease surface. Cover; let rise till almost double, about 1¼ hours. Punch down.

Turn out onto lightly floured surface and divide dough in thirds; form into balls. Let rest 10 minutes. Roll each ball to a 16-inch long rope. Line up the 3 ropes, 1 inch apart, on greased baking sheet. Braid loosely, beginning in the middle and working toward ends. Pinch ends together and tuck under. Cover; let rise till almost double, 40 minutes. Brush with milk and sprinkle with sugar, if desired. Bake at 375° for 20 to 25 minutes.

Rum Pudding (Denmark)

In mixing bowl add ¼ teaspoon salt to 3 egg yolks; beat till thick and lemon-colored. Gradually beat in 6 tablespoons sugar. In saucepan soften 1 envelope unflavored gelatin in ⅔ cup milk; heat till gelatin dissolves. Cool slightly. Add milk mixture gradually to egg yolk mixture, beating constantly. Add 3 tablespoons rum. Chill till partially set. Whip 1 cup whipping cream; fold into gelatin mixture. Turn into 6 individual molds. Chill till set. Unmold and serve with Raspberry Sauce. Makes 6 servings.

Raspberry Sauce: Combine ¼ cup sugar and 1 tablespoon cornstarch; stir in one 10-ounce package frozen raspberries, thawed, and ⅓ cup cold water. Cook and stir till thickened and bubbly; boil 2 minutes. Sieve; chill.

Grandmother's Jelly Cookies (Sweden)

Pretty as well as good-tasting—

> 1 cup butter or margarine
> ¾ cup sugar
> 1 egg
> 3 cups sifted all-purpose flour
> ½ teaspoon salt
> 2 slightly beaten egg whites
> ½ cup finely chopped, blanched almonds
> ¼ to ⅓ cup sugar
> ¼ to ½ cup currant jelly

Cream together butter or margarine and the ¾ cup sugar till light and fluffy. Beat in egg. Sift together flour and salt; add to creamed mixture. Mix thoroughly.

Divide dough in half; roll one half to ⅛-inch thickness on a lightly floured board. Cut into 2½-inch circles. Roll out remaining half of dough to ⅛-inch thickness; cut with 2-inch scalloped cookie cutter. Using a very small cutter or thimble, cut a 1-inch circle out of center of smaller rounds. Brush tops of smaller rounds with egg whites; sprinkle with almonds and remaining sugar.

Place cookies on *ungreased* cookie sheets; bake at 375° for 8 to 10 minutes. Cool. Place small amount of jelly in center of larger cookies. Top with smaller cookies; press together. Makes about 3 dozen cookies.

An unusual shape coupled with a delicious spicy flavor make Finnish Viipuri Twist an extra-special yeast bread worth making.

Uppakrakakor (Sweden)

> 1 cup butter or margarine
> ½ cup sifted confectioners' sugar
> 1¾ cups sifted all-purpose flour
> ⅔ cup cornstarch
> 1 slightly beaten egg
> ½ cup chopped, blanched almonds
> 2 teaspoons granulated sugar

Cream together butter and confectioners' sugar till light and fluffy. Sift together flour and cornstarch; add to creamed mixture, blending thoroughly. Chill 30 minutes. (Dough should remain chilled while working, so remove only 1 quarter from refrigerator at a time.) Roll out to ⅛-inch thickness on floured surface; cut into 2-inch circles. Place on *ungreased* cookie sheets. Fold each cookie almost in half so edges do not quite meet. Brush tops with beaten egg; sprinkle with almonds and granulated sugar. Bake at 350° till cookies are light, golden yellow, about 10 minutes. Makes about 4½ dozen.

Swedish cookies include Brandy Rings (see *Brandy* for recipe), Uppakrakakor, Rye Cookies, and Grandmother's Jelly Cookies.

Aebleskiver (Danish Doughnuts)

Especially good with coffee—

In mixing bowl sift together 1 cup sifted all-purpose flour, 1 teaspoon sugar, ½ teaspoon baking soda, ¼ teaspoon salt, and ¼ teaspoon ground cardamom. Combine 1¼ cups buttermilk, 2 well-beaten egg yolks, and ½ teaspoon vanilla. Stir half buttermilk mixture into dry ingredients in mixing bowl; mix just till smooth. Stir in remaining liquid. Fold 2 stiffly beaten egg whites into batter.

To cook doughnuts heat aebleskiver pan* (a special pan with a small cup for each doughnut) over low heat; oil each cup lightly. Spoon 2 tablespoons batter into each cup. Cook till bubbles form and edges appear dry, about 2 to 3 minutes. Gently turn with 2 wooden picks. Cook till second side is golden brown, about 2 to 3 minutes. Repeat with remaining batter. Dust with confectioners' sugar and serve hot with applesauce or jelly. Makes 20.

*Batter can also be cooked on lightly greased griddle, using 2 tablespoons per pancake.

Lucia Braid (Sweden)

Serve this delicious bread as a Christmas treat—

> 2 packages active dry yeast
> 5 to 5⅓ cups sifted all-purpose flour
> ½ teaspoon ground cardamom
> 1⅓ cups milk
> ½ cup shortening
> ½ cup sugar
> 1½ teaspoons salt
> 2 eggs
> . . .
> Confectioners' Sugar Glaze
> Walnut halves
> Red and green candied cherries

In large mixer bowl combine active dry yeast, 2½ *cups* of the all-purpose flour, and cardamom. In saucepan heat milk, shortening, sugar, and salt just till warm, stirring occasionally to melt shortening. Add to dry mixture in mixer bowl; add eggs. Beat at low speed with electric mixer for ½ minute, scraping sides of bowl constantly. Beat 3 minutes at high speed. By hand, stir in enough of the remaining all-purpose flour to make a soft dough.

Turn dough out onto well-floured surface. Knead till smooth and elastic, about 8 to 10 minutes. Place dough in lightly greased bowl; turn once to grease surface. Cover; let rise in warm place till double, about 2 hours. Punch down. Divide dough in half; cover and let rest 10 minutes. Divide one half of the dough into 4 parts. Roll 3 parts of dough into 20-inch strands; braid. Carefully place braid around greased 6-ounce juice can on greased baking sheet. Seal ends together to form continuous braid. Divide fourth part of dough in half. Shape into two 20-inch strands and twist together. Place twist on top of braid. Repeat with remaining half of dough.

Let dough rise in warm place till double, about 1 hour. Bake at 350° till bread is golden, about 25 minutes. Carefully remove the juice can. While wreaths are still warm, brush with Confectioners' Sugar Glaze. Decorate tops with walnut halves and red and green candied cherries. Makes 2 wreaths.

Confectioners' Sugar Glaze: Add enough milk *or* light cream to 2 cups sifted confectioners' sugar to make of spreading consistency. Add 1 teaspoon vanilla and dash salt; mix well.

Finnish Viipuri Twist

In large mixer bowl combine 2 packages active dry yeast, 2½ cups sifted all-purpose flour, ½ teaspoon ground cardamom, and ½ teaspoon ground nutmeg. Heat together 2 cups milk, ¼ cup butter or margarine, ¾ cup sugar, and 1 teaspoon salt just till warm, stirring occasionally to melt butter. Add to dry ingredients in mixer bowl; beat ½ minute on low speed of electric mixer, scraping bowl constantly. Beat 3 minutes at high speed. By hand, beat in enough of 3 to 3¼ cups all-purpose flour to make a moderately stiff dough. Turn out onto lightly floured surface. Knead till smooth and elastic, about 5 to 8 minutes.

Place in greased bowl, turning once to grease surface. Cover and let rise till double, 1 to 1½ hours. Punch down; divide into 3 parts and let rest for about 10 minutes.

On floured surface, shape 1 part of the dough into a roll 36 inches long. Cross ends of dough to form a circle, having each end extend about 6 inches. Holding ends of dough toward center of circle, twist together twice. Press ends together and tuck under center of top of circle, forming a pretzel-shaped roll. Place on greased baking sheet. Repeat with 2 remaining parts of dough. Let rise again till almost double, about 45 minutes. Bake at 375° for about 20 minutes. Stir together 1 slightly beaten egg and 1 tablespoon water; brush on hot breads. Makes 3 loaves.

Stag's Antlers (Norway)

Delicately cardamom flavored—

In mixing bowl cream ½ cup butter or margarine and ¾ cup sugar till light and fluffy. Beat in 2 egg yolks and 1 whole egg. Add ¼ cup milk and ½ teaspoon ground cardamom. Sift together 2¼ cups sifted all-purpose flour, ½ cup cornstarch, 1 teaspoon baking soda, and ½ teaspoon salt. Add to egg mixture; blend thoroughly. Chill dough thoroughly.

Roll dough out on lightly floured surface to ¼-inch thickness. Cut into 2x1-inch strips. Transfer to *ungreased* cookie sheets. Cut 2 slits in each strip, ¾ inch from each end and cutting across a little more than half the width of the strip. Curve to open slits. Bake at 350° till golden, 10 to 12 minutes. Sprinkle with sugar. Cool. Store in airtight container. Makes 72.

Rye Cookies (Sweden)

  ½ cup butter or margarine
  ⅓ cup sugar
  ½ cup rye flour
  ½ cup whole wheat flour
  ½ cup sifted all-purpose flour
  ¼ teaspoon baking powder

Cream together butter and sugar till light and fluffy. Stir in rye flour and whole wheat flour. Sift together all-purpose flour, baking powder, and ¼ teaspoon salt; stir into creamed mixture. Gradually add 2 to 3 tablespoons cold water, mixing just till moistened. Shape into a ball. Roll cookie dough out on lightly floured surface to ⅛-inch thickness.

Cut into 2½-inch rounds. Using a thimble, cut a ½-inch circle, just off-center, from each cookie. Prick surface with fork, if desired. Place on *ungreased* cookie sheet. Bake at 375° till lightly browned, about 10 to 12 minutes. Cool slightly before removing from cookie sheet. Makes 4 to 5 dozen.

Sandbakkels (Norway)

  1 cup butter or margarine
  1 cup sugar
  1 egg
  1 teaspoon almond extract
  3 cups sifted all-purpose flour
  1 cup apricot preserves
  2 teaspoons lemon juice
  ¼ cup chopped red candied cherries
  ¼ cup toasted, sliced almonds

Thoroughly cream butter or margarine and sugar. Add egg and almond extract; beat well. Stir in sifted flour. Pinch off small ball of dough and place in center of 2½-inch sandbakkel mold*; with your thumb, press dough evenly and as thinly as possible over bottom and sides. Place molds on cookie sheet.

Bake at 350° till lightly browned, 12 to 14 minutes. Cool. To remove, invert mold; tap lightly. (Clean molds with dry cloth.)

Just before serving, combine preserves, lemon juice, and cherries. Place 1 teaspoon of mixture in each cookie tart. Stir in almonds or sprinkle over. Makes about 3½ dozen.

*They look like tiny, fluted, tart pans. If not available, use tiny foilware pans instead.

Smorgasbord

Mention of Scandinavian cookery almost invariably brings to mind the smorgasbord. In fact, an adaptation of this lavish meal is found in all the Scandinavian countries. For example, the special buffet meal called *voileinpapoyta* is the Finn's form of the smorgasbord. However, the true smorgasbord (literally bread and butter table) belongs to Sweden.

The traditional smorgasbord, which actually only dates back to the late 1800s, consists of dozens of dishes spread out on a large table. Considering the huge amount of food, it is not at all surprising that as the diner approaches the smorgasbord, he is often overwhelmed. A second look, however, shows that the typical smorgasbord selections can be broken down into four groups—herring dishes (such as pickled, smoked, marinated, and fried herring); other fish dishes and/or cold egg dishes (for example, smoked eel, jellied salmon, stuffed eggs, and fried salmon fins); cold meats and salads (including ham, roast beef, tongue, pickled onions, beets, and cucumbers), and hot dishes (Swedish meatballs, rice pudding, omelets, fried kidneys, stuffed onions, and fried mushrooms).

During the course of a smorgasbord, you should use four plates—one for each group of dishes. Although you will soon find that it's virtually an impossible task to sample every dish on the smorgasbord, you can easily taste a representative sample if, from the start, you will just remember to save room for the dishes yet to come.

Stuffed Celery

> Cream cheese, softened
> Blue cheese, crumbled
> Celery sticks
> Capers
> Canned pimiento, cut into
>   tiny diamonds

Beat together cream cheese and blue cheese (add to suit your taste) till fluffy. Stuff celery with cheese. Dot filled celery with capers and pimiento. Stand celery up around inverted tumbler. Hide glass with celery leaves.

Decorated Ham

> Canned ham, chilled
> Unpeeled cucumber
> Canned asparagus spears, chilled
> Canned pimiento strip
> Wedge of bread (about ⅓ of an
>   unsliced loaf)
> Lettuce
> Curly endive
> Radish roses
> Bright red apple
> Lettuce *or* individual vegetable
>   salads

Place chilled ham on large platter. Run tines of fork down cucumber, notching skin all around. Cut cucumber in ¼-inch slices, then cut slices in half. Stand these half-circles on edge, overlapping them, to make 2 parallel rows along top of ham at side edges.

Between cucumber rows center a bundle of 3 or 4 asparagus spears tied with pimiento. For a Yuletide touch, wrap 2 asparagus spears in 2 thin ham slices and stand on end to resemble a candle at center of each side of ham; hold in place with wooden picks.

For the backdrop, stand the wedge of bread on its smallest side with the long slope toward one end of the ham. Completely cover bread with lettuce and endive, tacking with wooden picks. Dot with radish roses, also held by wooden picks. Nestle bright red apple between greenery and ham. Garnish platter with lettuce or individual vegetable salads.

Swedish Brown Beans

> 1 pound Swedish brown beans
> 3 inches stick cinnamon
> ⅓ cup brown sugar
> ¼ cup vinegar
> 2 tablespoons dark corn syrup

Rinse beans; drain. Add 6 cups cold water; cover and let stand overnight. (Or bring water and beans slowly to boiling; simmer 2 minutes. Cover; let stand 1 hour.) Add cinnamon and 1½ teaspoons salt. Cover; simmer till beans are about tender, 1½ to 2 hours. Add sugar and vinegar. Cook, uncovered, till beans are tender and liquid is desired consistency, 30 minutes; stir occasionally. Add syrup. Serves 6.

Quick Swedish Meatballs

Thoroughly combine 2 pounds ground beef, 2 cups soft bread crumbs, two 3-ounce packages cream cheese, ¼ cup *dry* onion soup mix, ½ teaspoon salt, ½ teaspoon ground nutmeg, and ½ cup milk. Shape into 40 small balls.

Brown in large skillet, shaking skillet to keep balls round. Cover and cook 20 to 25 minutes. Remove meatballs. Drain off fat, leaving ¼ cup fat in skillet; blend in 2 tablespoons all-purpose flour. Stir in 2 cups milk all at once. Cook and stir till thickened and bubbly. Return meatballs to skillet; cover and cook till heated through. Serves 10 to 12.

Individual characteristics

Even though Denmark, Norway, Sweden, and Finland are generally lumped together as Scandinavia, each of these four countries still retains a character of its own. This individuality shows up in cookery where there are particular foods and techniques that are typical only of one or the other of the Scandinavian countries.

For example, the Danes are known for their extensive use of the butter, cream, and eggs that are so plentiful there. In fact, they put their own stamp on breads, pastries, cookies, soups, and almost every other dish by adding butter or cream.

One of the characteristics of Norwegian cooking is the generous use of sour cream. Much as the Danes use butter and sweet cream, the Norwegians use sour cream in soups, sauces, salads, porridge, waffles, and meat and vegetable dishes.

Swedish cooks are artists in using subtle touches to individualize the foods they prepare. They add a touch of beet juice to the cream used to dress herring or a bit of sugar to give just the right finishing touch to a creamy sauce. They also put a little cream in their meat croquettes and cold mashed potatoes in meatballs to give the finished product a light texture. Sauces are important dress-ups also, especially for vegetables, poultry, meat, or fish.

Finland's forests yield many foods, including mushrooms, which the Finns particularly enjoy. From spring to autumn, the Finns gather large quantities of mushrooms from the over fifty edible varieties that are found in the Finnish countryside. These tasty delicacies are often pickled, fried, or used in soups, sauces, salads, stews, and main dishes. (See *Danish Cookery, Norwegian Cookery, Swedish Cookery* for additional information.)

SCHAUM TORTE (*shoum' tôrt'*) – A dessert made of layers of crushed fruit and meringue shells. (See also *Torte*.)

SCHAV (*shchäv*) – A pale green soup, Russian and Magyar in origin, which is now primarily associated with Jewish cookery. It is made of water, sorrel (sour grass) leaves, lemon juice, a well-beaten egg, and seasonings. Served either hot or cold, schav is popularly garnished with a dollop of sour cream, sliced hard-cooked egg, lemon or lime slices, or snipped parsley. (See also *Jewish Cookery*.)

SCHMALTZ, SCHMALZ (*shmälts, shmôlts*) – The Jewish word for rendered fat of meat animals or poultry. It usually refers to rendered chicken fat, and is of two types— one simply salted for use in cake baking and one flavored with onion. The former is made by melting small bits of chicken fat over very low heat. As melted fat accumulates, it is poured off and strained. The fat for flavored schmaltz is melted over low heat with chopped onion (and garlic if desired) and bits of chopped chicken skin. It is used to add piquancy to meat or vegetables dishes. Schmaltz should be kept tightly covered and refrigerated. (See also *Jewish Cookery*.)

SCHNECKEN (*shnek' uhn*) – Fruit- or nut-filled sweet rolls, shaped like snails.

SCHNITZ (*shnits*) – The Pennsylvania Dutch name for dried sliced apples. (See also *Pennsylvania Dutch Cookery*.)

SCHNITZ AND KNEPP (*shnits' uhn kuh nep', -knep'*) – A Pennsylvania Dutch main dish prepared with dried apple slices called *schnitz*, dumplings called *knepp*, and ham or pork. The dish is also sometimes made without the meat. (See also *Pennsylvania Dutch Cookery*.)

SCHNITZEL *(shnit' suhl)* — The German and Austrian word for a cutlet, usually veal, that has been dipped in egg, then in bread crumbs, and finally sautéed or fried in fat before it is seasoned and garnished.

An American version of schnitzel includs a filled ham slice coated and fried in shortening. (See also *Wiener Schnitzel*.)

Filled Ham Schnitzel

Mushrooms and parsley make up the filling—

> 1 6-ounce can chopped mushrooms,
>   drained and finely chopped
> 3 tablespoons butter or margarine
> 2 tablespoons snipped parsley
> 1 tablespoon all-purpose flour
> 8 slices boiled ham
> 1 slightly beaten egg
> ½ cup all-purpose flour
> ½ cup fine dry bread crumbs
> 3 tablespoons shortening

Brown mushrooms in butter with parsley. Add 1 tablespoon flour; cook and stir for 2 minutes. Cool. Spread mixture on one half of each slice of ham. Fold other half over; press to secure. Dip schnitzel in egg, then in ½ cup flour, back into egg, and then in crumbs. Brown on both sides in hot shortening. Makes 4 servings.

SCONE — A plain or sweet biscuitlike tea cake made of baking powder dough that is enriched with eggs and milk or cream. A Scottish food, scones originally were made with oatmeal and baked on a griddle.

Prepare scones for baking in the oven or on a griddle by first rolling the dough to an even thickness. Then, cut the dough into any one of a number of shapes—circles, diamonds, or wedges.

For soft sides, allow the sides of the scones to touch during baking and split them apart after baking. For crisp sides, bake the scones separately without letting the sides touch. In either case, brush the top of the scones before baking with a beaten egg or milk. This gives them a rich, golden color. Turn scones that are baked on a griddle so as to allow them to cook through completely.

Score meats by slashing through the fat layer on the edge just to but not through the meat. This prevents curling during cooking.

Tea Scones

> 2 cups sifted all-purpose flour
> 2 tablespoons sugar
> 3 teaspoons baking powder
> 6 tablespoons butter
> 1 slightly beaten egg
> ½ cup milk

Sift together dry ingredients and ½ teaspoon salt. Cut in butter till mixture resembles coarse crumbs. Add egg and milk, stirring till dough follows fork around bowl. Knead on floured surface 15 times; cut in half. Shape each half into ball; pat to circle ½ inch thick and 6 inches in diameter; cut in 8 wedges.

Place the wedges on an *ungreased* baking sheet, without allowing sides to touch. Brush with egg, if desired. Bake at 425° till deep golden brown, 12 to 15 minutes. Makes 16.

SCOOP — **1.** A shovel- or ladle-type utensil made of plastic, metal, or wood and designed for dipping food from one container to another. Examples include ice cream scoops and scoops for coffee, sugar, flour, and other ground or powdered ingredients. **2.** To dip or hollow out.

When filling fruits or vegetables, such as baked potatoes, tomatoes, oranges, or green peppers with seasoned food mixtures, use a spoon to scoop out the insides of foods first. (See also *Utensil*.)

Run tines of fork lengthwise down unpeeled cucumber, all around, breaking through skin. Slice scored cucumber in thin slices.

SCORE—To make shallow slits or slashes partway through the outer surface of food for functional or decorative purposes.

Scoring the fat layer of meat allows fat drainage and crisping of the meat during cooking. To score steaks, chops, or ham slices, use a sharp knife to slash through the fat layer on the edge just to the meat. This prevents the meat from curling and folding as it cooks.

When scoring less tender cuts of meat such as beef flank steak or round steak, cut slashes in the long, fibrous surface in an overall diamond pattern. This shortens the long meat fibers, making the meat more tender and easier to chew. Scoring the surface of meat enables a marinade to better penetrate the meat, making it more flavorful and tender.

Many homemakers score foods to make their meals more appetizing. To give a ham a decorative appearance, cut an overall pattern of squares or diamonds through the outside fat layer. It is also quite easy to decorate fruits and vegetables by scoring them lengthwise. Simply use the tines of a fork to break through the skins of the fruit or vegetables, then run the fork down the fruit. Slice and use the fruit or vegetable in salads, as a garnish, or as a relish.

SCOTCH BROTH—A thin soup of Scottish origin made of mutton or lamb, barley, and/or mixed vegetables. (See also *Soup.*)

Scotch Broth

Combine and simmer lamb or mutton, barley, and mixed vegetables to make this hearty soup—

> 1 pound boneless lamb, cut in
>   2-inch cubes
> 4 cups water
> 1 teaspoon salt
> 1 bay leaf, crushed
> 2 whole cloves
> 3 sprigs parsley
> ½ cup chopped onion
>   • • •
> ¼ cup pearl barley
> ½ cup diced carrots
> ¼ cup diced celery
> ¼ cup diced turnip

In 3-quart saucepan combine lamb, water, salt, bay leaf, cloves, parsley, and ¼ *cup* of the chopped onion. Bring mixture to boiling; reduce heat and simmer, covered, till meat is tender, about 2 hours. Remove meat from soup; cut into small pieces. Set the meat aside.

Strain stock; add barley. Simmer mixture for 30 minutes. Add carrots, celery, turnip, and remaining chopped onion. Cook till vegetables are tender, about 30 minutes longer. Add meat; heat through. Makes 4 or 5 servings.

SCOTCH HAM—A cook-before-eating style of ham that is cured but not smoked. The ham is marketed as a regional specialty by New England processors. Because it is processed with a sweet pickle brine, it also known as sweet pickle ham.

Scotch ham has a delicate, pink color and a mild flavor. It is occasionally used to prepare the familiar boiled dinner with potatoes and carrots. (See also *Ham.*)

SCOTCH WHISKY—A Scottish-made whiskey based on malt barley. The distinctive, smoky flavor of Scotch whisky is developed by drying the barley over open peat fires. Before bottling, Scotch whisky imported by United States markets is aged in wooden casks for at least four years.

Scotch whisky of the past differed profoundly from what most people recognize as Scotch whisky today. Originally, the whisky was distilled solely from germinated or malted barley and produced an intense-flavored liquor. This is still made and sold in Scotland. Now, however, Scotch whisky, also called Scotch, is most often a milder blend of malt and grain whiskies, which appeals to more palates.

These two forms of Scotch whisky are well accepted today, but in years past there was considerable contention in Scotland over just what whisky was. The Scots of the Highlands, originators of Scotch whisky, have always distilled the malt whisky. Although its potency was well liked by Highlanders, more sophisticated individuals in Great Britain were not fond of the strong flavor. With the development of patent stills, which enabled distillation of grain blends, milder Scotch whiskies were produced, much to the dismay of the Highlanders. In the 1905 court decision of the "What is whisky" case, however, the patent distillers won a long-fought battle. Ninety-nine percent of all Scotch that is exported today consists of this grain-blended type.

Half the Scotch produced is consumed by people of the United States. Popular drinks include Scotch and soda, Scotch on the rocks, Rob Roy, Scotch mist, and rusty nail. (See also *Whiskey.*)

Season Scrambled Eggs with Tomatoes with dried oregano leaves and parsley flakes for a new and interesting breakfast idea.

Cook scrambled eggs over low heat. Lift and turn eggs with a wide spatula so uncooked mixture goes to the bottom of the skillet.

SCRAMBLE—1. A preparation method in which ingredients are stirred together while cooking. **2.** A cereal snack that gets its name from items that are tossed together.

The term is most commonly associated with stirring beaten eggs with milk and seasonings while cooking in butter. The cooked dish is called scrambled eggs.

Preparation methods for scrambled eggs vary a great deal. For creamy, golden-yellow scrambled eggs, beat the eggs with the liquid, usually milk or light cream, before cooking. For a flecked yellow and white appearance, break the eggs in a skillet and stir while cooking.

For either method, the eggs are usually cooked in a skillet. However, for softer, less rich scrambled eggs, omit the butter and cook the egg mixture in the top of a double boiler. This method takes about twice as long. Calorie watchers can scramble eggs in nonstick pans without butter.

If the family seems to lose interest in your scrambled eggs, vary the flavor by tossing in herbs and seasonings such as parsley, chives, or thyme. Vegetables such as tomato wedges, green pepper strips, or sliced mushrooms also add flavor and color. Add a delectable flavor by cooking scrambled eggs in bacon drippings. For hearty brunches add diced, cooked meats such as chicken or ham. Or dribble melted cheese over the scrambled eggs. (See *Cereal, Egg* for additional information.)

Scrambled Eggs with Tomatoes

    6 eggs
    ¼ cup milk
    ½ teaspoon salt
    ¼ teaspoon dried oregano leaves,
        crushed
    ¼ teaspoon dried parsley flakes
        Dash pepper
    2 tablespoons butter or margarine
    1 8-ounce can tomatoes, drained
        and cut up

Combine eggs, milk, salt, crushed oregano, parsley flakes, and pepper. Beat with fork till mixture is smooth and yellow. Melt butter in skillet over medium heat. Add egg mixture and cook, lifting mixture gently from bottom of pan with spatula. When eggs are nearly done, lightly fold in tomato pieces; turn out immediately onto heated platter. Makes 4 servings.

Chicken Scramble

    8 beaten eggs
    2 ounces *natural* Cheddar cheese,
        shredded (½ cup)
    ¼ cup milk
    ½ teaspoon salt
        Dash pepper
    3 tablespoons butter or margarine
    1 cup cooked chicken, cut in
        julienne strips
    1 tablespoon snipped chives

In bowl combine first 5 ingredients. Set electric skillet at 320°; melt butter in skillet. Add chicken and chives; cook and stir 3 minutes. Add egg-cheese mixture. Cook, stirring occasionally, till eggs are set. Makes 6 servings.

SCRAPE—To rub over food with a sharp or moderately blunt instrument to remove the outer coating. Scraping skins off new potatoes or carrots are examples.

SCRAPER—A long-handled, rubber-bladed instrument, firm but flexible, used to scrape food from containers without scratching them. Often called rubber spatula, a scraper is also good for folding in beaten egg whites and for folding omelets.

SCRAPPLE—A cooked meat product originated by thrifty Pennsylvania Dutch farmers to use up the small bits of pork left after butchering. The liver, tongue, meaty bones, and all scraps left from butchering are thoroughly boiled, producing a broth. Seasoning the mixture is an individual part of the preparation. Formerly, the Germans used buckwheat flour to thicken scrapple, although the Pennsylvania Dutch preferred a combination of buckwheat and cornmeal. Now, cornmeal is usually used.

After the scrapple has been boiled to a mushlike stage, it is packed into loaf pans to set, then chilled. At serving time, it is sliced and sautéed or fried. Sometimes, the slices are dipped in eggs and a crumb mixture before frying. Although scrapple is usually served with hot maple or brown sugar syrup, some people prefer it with catsup or hot fruit.

Scrapple is bought ready to fry, canned or packaged, as Philadelphia scrapple. (See also *Pennsylvania Dutch Cookery*.)

Sausage Scrapple

    2 pounds bulk pork sausage
    1 14½-ounce can evaporated milk
        (1⅔ cups)
    3 cups water
    1½ cups yellow cornmeal
    ½ teaspoon salt
        All-purpose flour *or* cornflake
        crumbs
    2 beaten eggs
    3 to 4 tablespoons shortening
        Syrup

Brown sausage slowly, breaking it up into small pieces; drain off excess fat. Combine milk and water. Add 4 cups of the milk mixture to sausage. Reserve remaining milk mixture. Heat sausage mixture to boiling; slowly stir in cornmeal and salt. Cook 5 minutes, stirring constantly. Pour into greased 9x5x3-inch loaf pan. Chill the mixture till firm.

Unmold and cut into ¼-inch slices. Dip in flour *or* cornflake crumbs. Combine eggs and remaining milk mixture. Dip slices in egg mixture, then in flour or crumbs again. In skillet brown in hot shortening on both sides. Serve hot with warm syrup. Serves 10 to 12.

SCRIPTURE CAKE—A rich cake made entirely from ingredients that are mentioned in the *Holy Bible,* such as raisins and nuts. Old-fashioned recipes for this cake carried the verse recipes as well as, or often in place of, the ingredient listings.

Scripture Cake

½ cup Judges 5:25
¾ cup Jeremiah 6:20
2¼ cups I Kings 4:22
1 teaspoon Amos 4:5
    Dash Leviticus 2:13
    II Chronicles 9:9
3 Jeremiah 17:11
½ cup Judges 4:19
⅓ cup I Samuel 14:25
1 cup I Samuel 30:12
1 cup Nahum 3:12
½ cup Numbers 17:8

In large mixer bowl cream Judges 5:25 (butter or margarine); blend in Jeremiah 6:20 (molasses). Sift together I Kings 4:22 (sifted all-purpose flour); Amos 4:5 (baking powder); Leviticus 2:13 (salt); and II Chronicles 9:9 (½ teaspoon ground cinnamon, ¼ teaspoon ground cloves, and ⅛ teaspoon ground ginger). Combine Jeremiah 17:11 (beaten eggs); Judges 4:19 (sour milk *or* buttermilk); and I Samuel 14:25 (honey). Stir to combine.

Add the egg mixture and the sifted dry ingredients alternately to creamed mixture. Mix well. Stir in I Samuel 30:12 (raisins); Nahum 3:12 (chopped figs); and Numbers 17:8 (chopped almonds). Turn mixture into greased and lightly floured 9x5x3-inch loaf pan. Bake at 325° for 1¼ to 1½ hours. Let cool in pan 10 minutes; turn out. When the cake has cooled completely, wrap and store overnight.

SCROD *(skrod)*—A young cod or haddock. This term describes the market size rather than a species. The young fish averages in weight from 1½ to 2½ pounds.

The meat is tender, white, and flaky. Delicate scrod flavor combines well with seasonings such as curry and is delicious baked, broiled, or used in chowders. Scrod is popular in Europe and on the east coast of the United States. (See also *Cod.*)

Curried Scrod

1½ pounds fresh or frozen scrod
    fillets (young haddock or cod)
½ cup chopped onion
2 tablespoons butter or margarine
1 to 1½ teaspoons curry powder
2 tablespoons all-purpose flour
¾ teaspoon salt
1 cup milk
2 tablespoons chopped, canned
    pimiento
3 cups hot cooked rice

Thaw frozen fillets. Cut into 4 or 5 portions. Place fillets in an 11¾x7½x1¾-inch baking dish. Cook onion in butter till tender but not brown. Stir in curry powder; heat 1 minute. Blend in flour and salt. Add milk all at once. Cook and stir till thickened and bubbly. Stir in pimiento. Pour over fish. Bake, uncovered, at 350° till fish flakes easily when tested with a fork, about 25 minutes. Spoon sauce over fish once or twice during baking. Serve with hot rice. Makes 4 or 5 servings.

SCUP *(skup)*—A type of porgy, a fish of the eastern United States. (See also *Porgy.*)

SCUPPERNONG *(skup' uhr nong', -nong')*—**1.** A sweet, thick-skinned, greenish yellow grape of the muscadine variety that grows well in the southern United States. The fruit is excellent for use in grape jams. **2.** A sweet, rich, white wine made from scuppernong grapes. (See also *Grape.*)

SEA BASS—A saltwater fish found along the east and west coasts of North America. The sea bass, also called blackfish, is a lean fish with firm, sweet, white flesh. It ranges in size from ½ to 4 pounds.

There are two other types of sea bass—the white sea bass, which weighs up to 50 pounds, and the black sea bass, which weighs from 50 to 600 pounds.

Although popular as a game fish, sea bass also are caught commercially and sold whole, or cut in fillets or steaks.

This fish can be boiled, fried, or steamed. With butter added, it also may be baked or broiled. A 3½-ounce uncooked portion contains 96 calories. (See also *Bass.*)

Barbecued Bass Steaks

    2 pounds fresh or frozen bass
         steaks
  ⅓ cup salad oil
    1 tablespoon sesame seed, toasted
    1 tablespoon lemon juice
    1 tablespoon wine vinegar
    1 tablespoon soy sauce
  ½ teaspoon salt

If using frozen fish, thaw. Cut into 6 portions. Place in single layer in shallow dish. Combine remaining ingredients. Pour over fish. Marinate 30 minutes at room temperature; turn once. Remove fish; reserve marinade.

    Place fish in *well-greased*, wire broiler basket. Grill over *medium-hot* coals for 10 minutes. Turn and baste with marinade. Grill till fish flakes easily when tested with a fork, 5 to 8 minutes longer. Makes 6 servings.

Broiled Bass Steaks

    2 pounds fresh or frozen bass steaks
      or other fish steaks
  ½ cup catsup
  ¼ cup salad oil
  ¼ cup lemon juice
    1 teaspoon instant minced onion
    1 teaspoon Worcestershire sauce
    1 teaspoon prepared mustard
  ½ teaspoon garlic salt
  ¼ teaspoon salt

Thaw frozen steaks. Cut into 6 portions. Place fish in a single layer in shallow dish. Combine remaining ingredients. Pour sauce over fish; let stand 1 hour at room temperature, turning once or twice. Remove fish; reserve sauce.

    Place fish in a single layer on greased rack of broiler pan. Broil about 4 inches from heat till fish flakes easily when tested with a fork, about 10 to 15 minutes. Baste with reserved sauce several times during broiling. Serves 6.

SEA FOAM—A divinity-type candy made of brown sugar syrup and beaten egg whites, sometimes with nuts added. The flavor of sea foam candy has been adapted to cake frosting by using brown sugar in Seven Minute Frosting. (See also *Candy*.)

Sea Foam

Have a friend help you make this candy—

      Butter or margarine
  1¾ cups light brown sugar
   ¾ cup granulated sugar
   ¼ cup light corn syrup
   ¼ teaspoon salt
   ½ cup water
    2 egg whites
    1 teaspoon vanilla
   ½ cup broken pecans (optional)

Butter sides of heavy 1½-quart saucepan. In it combine light brown sugar, granulated sugar, light corn syrup, salt, and water. Cook, stirring constantly, till sugars dissolve and mixture comes to boiling. Cook to hard-ball stage (260°) without stirring. Remove from heat.

    Immediately beat egg whites till stiff peaks form. Pour hot syrup in a thin stream over beaten egg whites, beating constantly at high speed on electric mixer. Add vanilla.

    Continue beating till mixture forms soft peaks and begins to lose gloss, 10 minutes. Stir in broken pecans, if desired. Let stand about 2 minutes; drop by rounded teaspoons onto waxed paper. Makes 2 to 3 dozen pieces.

Sea Foam Frosting

Top your best cake with this candylike frosting—

    2 unbeaten egg whites
  1½ cups brown sugar
    2 teaspoons light corn syrup *or*
      ¼ teaspoon cream of tartar
  ⅓ cup cold water
     Dash salt
    1 teaspoon vanilla

Place all ingredients *except* vanilla in top of double boiler (not over heat); beat 1 minute with electric or rotary beater. Place over, but not touching, boiling water and cook, beating constantly, till frosting forms stiff peaks, about 7 minutes (don't overcook).

    Remove from boiling water. Pour into mixing bowl, if desired. Add vanilla and beat till of spreading consistency, about 2 minutes. Frosts tops and sides of two 8- or 9-inch layers, top of 13x9-inch cake, or 2 dozen cupcakes.

SEAFOOD

SEAFOOD—Saltwater fish or shellfish eaten as food. The term seafood in menus and cookery refers mainly to shellfish. Snails, turtles, frogs, octopuses, and squid are sometimes included in this broad category of seafood because they are prepared like fish and shellfish. (See *Fish, Shellfish* for additional information.)

Clam-Haddock Chowder

¼ cup all-purpose flour
¼ cup shortening, melted
1 teaspoon curry powder
4 cups clam juice
3 cups fish stock *or* water
½ cup chili sauce
¼ cup tomato purée

. . .

½ cup diced celery
½ cup chopped onions
1 teaspoon salt
    Dash pepper
⅛ teaspoon saffron
⅛ teaspoon dried thyme leaves, crushed
⅛ teaspoon dried rosemary leaves, crushed
½ pound haddock, diced
½ cup peeled, diced potatoes
¼ cup diced leeks

. . .

1½ cups minced clams
1 cup cooked tomatoes
¾ cup diced green pepper
1 clove garlic, minced
1 teaspoon snipped parsley
⅓ cup Madeira *or* sherry wine
12 soft-shell clams, cooked

Blend all-purpose flour, melted shortening, and curry powder in a deep saucepan; cook 2 minutes, stirring constantly. Gradually add clam juice, fish stock or water, chili sauce, and tomato purée. Cook mixture until thickened and bubbly, stirring constantly.

Add celery, onions, salt, pepper, saffron, thyme, and rosemary. Simmer 15 minutes. Add haddock, potatoes, and leeks; cook 15 minutes. Add minced clams, tomatoes, green pepper, and garlic; cook 15 minutes. Remove mixture from heat; add snipped parsley, Madeira or sherry, and cooked clams. Makes 6 to 8 servings.

Shore Dinner

Partially cook frozen lobster tails by simmering in salted water 10 minutes. With scissors, snip each lobster shell open, remove the meat, and cut in thirds. Peel and devein the shrimp, leaving last section of the shell and tail intact. String the following on rotating skewers: lobster chunks, shrimp, scallops, cherry tomatoes, and stuffed green olives.

Brush with lemon-butter (1 part lemon juice to 2 parts melted butter). Sprinkle with salt. Place rotating skewers on grill. Broil till the seafood is done, about 8 to 10 minutes, brushing frequently with lemon-butter. Before serving the food, sprinkle it with snipped parsley. Serve this dish piping hot with Tartar Sauce (see *Tartar Sauce* for recipe).

SEAFOOD SEASONING—A ground blend of ingredients used to flavor fish, shellfish, chowders, and sauces. Some of the ingredients included in commercial blends are salt, celery seed, mustard, thyme, ginger, peppers, allspice, and bay leaves.

Sprinkle this seasoning over fish and shellfish either before broiling, baking, and grilling or before serving. Enhance the flavor of dishes made with or served with fish and shellfish by adding seafood seasoning. Soups, chowders, stuffings, tartar sauce, Newburg sauce, and lemon-butter sauce can be flavored to taste.

Another spicy blend called shrimp boil or crab boil can be added to the water used to cook seafood, mainly shellfish.

SEAR—To brown food quickly. Searing, once used extensively, is done by cooking the food for a short time in a very hot oven or on top of the range at high heat. This forms a brown crust that has a good caramelized flavor. However, it has been found that meats roasted in a slow oven without searing retain their juices, shrink little, and have a browned, flavorful surface.

The first step in braising meats is not the same as searing. In braising, meats are browned *slowly* in a little fat.

SEASON—To add herbs and spices to enhance the basic character of a dish. Food should be seasoned carefully to develop a harmonious blend. Seasoning should enhance the dish's flavor, yet must not overpower the flavor of the main ingredient.

The recipe direction, "season to taste," means to add the herb or spice till the desired flavor is achieved. Begin with ¼ teaspoon for each 4 servings, 1 pound of meat, or 2 cups of sauce or vegetables. Then, if not enough, increase the amount gradually. When the desired level is reached, note total amount on recipe.

If a recipe calls for a seasoning, but no herbs or spices are specified, season with salt and pepper. Other seasonings also can be added according to the type of food and personal taste.

When to add seasonings

For full flavor, add seasonings during cooking rather than waiting until just before serving. If the food requires long cooking, add seasonings during the last half hour.

SEASONED PEPPER—A commercial blend of black pepper, sweet pepper, sugar, and spices. The ingredients and proportions vary from manufacturer to manufacturer. Some types of seasoned pepper have one predominant seasoning, for example, lemon pepper. Use it in place of black pepper for extra flavor. (See also *Pepper*.)

SEASONED SALT—A mixture of salt, spices, herbs, and various ingredients. Each manufacturer's blend differs, but sugar, onion, garlic, cornstarch, spices, and herbs are usually included in the formula.

Seasoned salt adds zip to vegetables, main dishes, and salads. The extra flavor quite often transforms an ordinary dish into an intriguing food.

If you like, make your own seasoned salt and vary the level of seasoning as desired. Homemade seasoning makes a very nice gift. Save empty spice bottles and shaker tops and fill with seasoned salt. Tie a ribbon around the neck and enclose a recipe for the salt or for a special way to use it. (See also *Salt*.)

Seasoned Salt

½ teaspoon dried marjoram leaves
½ teaspoon dried thyme leaves
⅛ teaspoon dillseed
⅓ cup salt
2 teaspoons paprika
1 teaspoon dry mustard
½ teaspoon curry powder
½ teaspoon garlic salt
½ teaspoon celery salt
¼ teaspoon onion powder

Place marjoram, thyme, and dillseed in blender container; crush by turning blender on and off. Add remaining ingredients and blend.

Or crush marjoram, thyme, and dillseed by hand; combine all ingredients in screw-top jar and shake till well combined. Makes ⅓ cup.

Country Potato Salad

1 pound small new potatoes (8 to 10), cooked and peeled
3 cups torn lettuce
2 hard-cooked eggs, diced
3 tablespoons thinly sliced green onion
6 slices bacon
¼ cup vinegar
1 teaspoon seasoned salt
¼ teaspoon celery seed

Leave very small potatoes whole; halve or quarter larger ones. In bowl, combine potatoes, lettuce, eggs, and onion. In skillet, cook bacon till crisp; drain, reserving ¼ cup drippings. Crumble bacon; add to salad.

To reserved drippings in skillet, add vinegar, seasoned salt, celery seed, and ⅛ teaspoon pepper. Heat mixture to boiling. Then, pour over potato mixture. Toss quickly; serve immediately. Makes 4 to 6 servings.

SEASONING—A small amount of spices, herbs, and condiments added to improve the taste, aroma, and feel of a food. Feel refers to temperature and consistency of the food. For instance, chili powder makes a dish hot and filé gives a slippery texture to foods. (See *Flavoring, Herb, Spice* for additional information.)

SEA TROUT—A lean, saltwater fish found chiefly in the Atlantic and Gulf coasts. They are also called weakfish.

There are several types of sea trout available on the market. The gray, spotted, and white sea trout are marketed both whole and filleted. The whole ones average about one or two pounds. All are white fleshed, tender, and delicate. The flavor varies from type to type.

Sea trout can be boiled, steamed, or fried. To bake or broil sea trout, brush the fish with butter or shortening before cooking. (See also *Fish*.)

SEAWEED—A collective term for a number of sea plants used in various capacities involving food and food preparation. Examples include carrageen or Irish moss and dulse. Seaweed is high in iodine and this is its most important nutritive contribution. Seaweed can be eaten as a relish or cooked and served as a vegetable. Sometimes it is used as a thickening agent in foods such as pudding.

SEC *(sek)*—The French word for dry which means unsweet when applied to still wines, and indicates that a small amount of sugar is present when used in connection with sparkling wines.

SECKEL PEAR *(sek' uhl, sik'-)*—A small, yellowish-brown variety of pear which originated near Philadelphia during the eighteenth century. This delectable pear is named after the Pennsylvania farmer who developed it. The sweet, spicy flavor and very firm texture of the Seckel pear make it particularly suitable for pickling and preserves. (See also *Pear*.)

SEEDCAKE—A sweet, butter cake or cookie of Irish and Scottish origin that contains caraway seed, sesame seed, or poppy seed. These seeds are mixed into the rich cake batter before baking.

SELF-RISING FLOUR—A commercial flour product to which leavening and salt have been added during processing. Self-rising flour can be used for quick breads (except popovers), pastry, cookies, and cakes (except sponge cakes). Because homemakers in the South bake more quick breads, this type of flour is more commonly found in that area. (See also *Flour*.)

SELTZER WATER—**1.** A naturally effervescent mineral water containing uncombined carbon dioxide from Nieder Seltzers of the Wiesbaden, Germany, district. **2.** Artificially carbonated effervescent water used in making soft drinks and in mixing alcoholic drinks. Seltzer water is often called carbonated water or soda water.

SEMISWEET CHOCOLATE—A type of chocolate suitable for cooking and eating that contains a small amount of sugar. Available packaged in bars, squares, or pieces, this chocolate is processed the same way as sweet chocolate save that less sweetening is added. Sometimes it is mint-flavored.

Semisweet chocolate melts easily during range-top cooking, yet holds its shape during baking at moderate oven temperatures. This is best illustrated by the intact pieces found in baked chocolate chip cookies and cakes. Melted semisweet chocolate squares are used for the chocolate coating on candies or for flavoring other types of candy. (See also *Chocolate*.)

Cake Mix Pronto Cookies

Full of chocolate pieces and nuts—

1 package 2-layer-size yellow cake mix
¼ cup butter or margarine, softened
⅓ cup milk
1 egg
½ teaspoon maple flavoring

. . .

1 6-ounce package semisweet chocolate pieces (1 cup)
½ cup chopped walnuts

Combine cake mix, butter or margarine, milk, egg, and maple flavoring; beat until smooth. Stir in semisweet chocolate pieces and chopped walnuts. Drop from teaspoon onto greased cookie sheet. Bake at 375° for about 12 minutes. Let stand a few seconds before removing from sheet. Makes about 4½ dozen cookies.

Mocha-Frosted Drops

 ½ cup shortening
 2 1-ounce squares unsweetened
  chocolate
 1 cup brown sugar
 1 egg
 1 teaspoon vanilla
 ½ cup buttermilk *or* sour milk
 1½ cups sifted all-purpose flour
 ½ teaspoon baking powder
 ½ teaspoon baking soda
 ¼ teaspoon salt
 ½ cup chopped walnuts
 1 6-ounce package semisweet
  chocolate pieces (1 cup)
 Mocha Frosting
 Walnut halves

Melt shortening and unsweetened chocolate together in a saucepan. Cool mixture for 10 minutes. Stir in the brown sugar. Beat in the egg, vanilla, and buttermilk *or* sour milk.

Sift together dry ingredients and add to chocolate mixture. Stir in nuts and chocolate pieces. Drop from teaspoon on greased cookie sheet. Bake at 375° about 10 minutes. Remove from pan and cool. Frost with Mocha Frosting. Top with walnut half, if desired. Makes 42.

Mocha Frosting: Cream ¼ cup butter, 2 tablespoons unsweetened cocoa powder, 2 teaspoons instant coffee powder, and dash salt. Beat in 2½ cups confectioners' sugar, 1½ teaspoons vanilla, and enough milk until the frosting is of spreading consistency.

Chocolate Chip Cake

Chopped chocolate is layered in batter—

 1 package 2-layer-size white cake
  mix
 1 6-ounce package semisweet
  chocolate pieces (1 cup)
 Sea Foam Frosting (See *Sea Foam*)

Prepare cake mix according to package directions. Reserving 3 tablespoons, chop remaining chocolate pieces. In 2 greased and lightly floured 8x1½- or 9x1½-inch round pans, alternate layers of batter with chopped chocolate. Bake as directed on package. Cool; frost with Seafoam Frosting. Dot with reserved chocolate.

Chocolate-Orange Rolls

Combine 1 package active dry yeast and 1½ cups sifted all-purpose flour. Heat together ½ cup milk, ¼ cup sugar, 2 tablespoons butter or margarine, and ½ teaspoon salt *just till warm*, stirring to melt butter. Add to dry mixture; add 2 eggs. Beat at low speed with electric mixer for ½ minute, scraping sides of bowl constantly. Beat 3 minutes at high speed. By hand, stir in ¾ to 1 cup sifted all-purpose flour, just enough to make a moderately soft dough.

Turn dough out onto lightly floured surface. Knead till smooth and elastic, about 4 to 5 minutes. Place dough in greased bowl; turn once to grease surface. Cover; let rise in warm place till double, about 1 hour. Punch down; turn out onto lightly floured surface. Cover; let dough rest for 10 minutes. Mix together ¼ cup sugar and 1 tablespoon shredded orange peel.

Roll dough to 15x10-inch rectangle. Spread with 2 tablespoons *softened* butter; sprinkle with the sugar mixture, then with ½ cup semisweet chocolate pieces. Roll up jelly-roll fashion, starting with the long side. Then, cut roll into 18 slices; place slices, cut side down, in two 9x9x2-inch baking pans (9 rolls in each pan). Let dough rise till nearly double, about 25 to 30 minutes. Bake at 375° till golden brown, about 12 to 15 minutes. Makes 18.

Chip-Cherry Fruitcake

 3 eggs
 1 cup sugar
 1½ cups sifted all-purpose flour
 1½ teaspoons baking powder
 ¼ teaspoon salt
 1 6-ounce package semisweet
  chocolate pieces (1 cup)
 2 cups chopped pecans
 1 8-ounce package dates, coarsely
  snipped (1⅓ cups)
 1 cup halved candied cherries

Beat eggs; stir in sugar. Sift together flour, baking powder, and salt; combine with chocolate pieces, pecans, dates, and candied cherries. Fold in egg-sugar mixture. Turn into greased and paper-lined 9x5x3-inch loaf pan. Place pan of water on bottom oven rack while baking. Bake on top rack at 325° for 1 hour. Cool slightly. Remove from pan; cool on rack.

SEMOLINA *(sem′ uh lē′ nuh)* – A coarse granulation of the durum wheat endosperm. It is made by grinding and bolting (sifting) durum wheat, separating the bran and germ to produce a granular product of not more than three percent flour. The term semolina comes from the Latin word *simila* which means finely ground wheat flour.

Semolina is used as the gluten in making high-quality pasta products. It is also used in making cereals, puddings, and soups. (See also *Durum Wheat.*)

SENEGALESE *(sen′ uh go lēz′, -les′, -guh-)* – A term used as part of a recipe title which indicates that curry is an ingredient.

SESAME SEED *(ses′ uh mē)* – A tiny, pale honey-colored seed with a mild, sweet, nut-like flavor produced from an annual tropical or subtropical herbaceous plant. Sesame is native to Asia, and has been cultivated in India, China, and Africa for thousands of years. Most likely the oldest crop grown for its edible oil, sesame dates back to 1600 B.C. Sesame seed, then known in Africa as *benne*, was first brought to America by slaves during the sixteenth and seventeenth centuries. Besides being edible, the seeds were thought to be tokens of good luck. The oil extracted from the seeds was often used for medicinal purposes.

The tiny seeds ripen inside a pod which bursts open upon maturation with a sharp pop. This sound, like the springing open of a door lock, may well be the source for Ali Baba's famous saying, "Open Sesame," which opened the door to riches in the tales of *The Thousand and One Nights.*

When the pods containing the sesame seed are well formed but green, they are harvested to minimize seed loss due to shattering. The crop is shucked like corn after being cut and tied in bundles.

Most sesame seed is hulled during processing. Whole sesame seed is available in most markets and sesame seed oil is found in specialty shops. It takes more than 12,000 seeds to make one ounce. Sesame seed oil, used as a cooking or salad oil as well as an ingredient in margarines and other shortenings, is produced by pressing the oil from the seeds.

Toasting sesame seed

Toasting brings out the flavor of sesame seeds and gives them a crunchy texture. If sprinkled atop breads or casseroles before baking, they will be toasted as the food cooks. If used as an ingredient, toast the seeds first.

To toast sesame seeds, spread seeds in a thin layer in a shallow, ungreased pan. Heat them in a preheated, moderate oven 10 to 15 minutes, stirring once or twice.

Sesame seed gives the distinctive flavor to the Turkish confection called halvah. You'll find both the flavor and texture of the seeds most enjoyable in cookies, on breads, with vegetables, chicken, and fish. Keep toasted sesame seed handy, too, to sprinkle onto salads, soups, and plain buttered vegetables just before serving.

Chicken–Sesame Balls

Combine two 5-ounce cans boned chicken, finely chopped; 1 tablespoon finely chopped onion; 2 tablespoons finely chopped, canned pimiento; 4 drops bottled hot pepper sauce; 1 tablespoon prepared mustard; and ¼ cup mayonnaise or salad dressing. Mix till thoroughly blended.

Form into balls, using about 1 teaspoon of mixture for each. Chill thoroughly, about 1 hour. Roll chilled balls in ¼ cup sesame seed, toasted. Makes 3 dozen appetizers.

Sesame Biscuits

Sift together 2 cups sifted all-purpose flour, 4 teaspoons baking powder, 2 teaspoons sugar, ½ teaspoon salt, and ½ teaspoon cream of tartar. Cut in ½ cup shortening till mixture is like coarse crumbs. Add ⅔ cup milk; stir only till dough follows fork around bowl.

Knead gently on lightly floured surface for 30 seconds. Roll ½ inch thick; cut in 2½-inch rounds. Place biscuits on *ungreased* baking sheet. Brush tops with a little milk. Sprinkle tops of biscuits with 1 tablespoon sesame seed. Bake biscuits at 450° for 10 to 12 minutes. Makes 16 biscuits.

Spiced Sesame Bars

Coat tiny bar cookies with sesame seed—

½ cup sifted all-purpose flour
¼ teaspoon salt
¼ teaspoon baking soda
¼ teaspoon ground allspice
¼ teaspoon ground mace
½ teaspoon ground cinnamon
1 egg
¾ cup brown sugar
3 tablespoons butter, melted
¼ cup sesame seed, toasted

Sift together flour, salt, soda, and spices; set aside. Beat egg; gradually add sugar and mix well. Stir in butter, then dry ingredients. Sprinkle *half* the sesame seed over bottom of greased 8x8x2-inch baking pan; pour in batter; top with remaining seed. Bake at 350° for 20 minutes. Let cool; cut in bars. Makes 32.

Sesame Cake

Sesame seed adds a delicate, nutlike flavor—

2¼ cups sifted cake flour
1½ cups sugar
3 teaspoons baking powder
½ teaspoon salt
¼ teaspoon ground mace
½ cup sesame seed, toasted
½ cup shortening
1¼ cups milk
2 eggs
Sea Foam Frosting (See *Sea Foam*)

Sift together dry ingredients; stir in sesame seed. Add shortening and ¾ *cup* milk. Beat 2 minutes on electric mixer. Add remaining milk and eggs; beat 1 minute. Pour into 2 greased and floured 8x1½-inch round pans. Bake at 350° for 25 minutes. Remove from pans. Frost the cooled cake with Seafoam Frosting.

SEVICHE *(sa vesh')* — A South American fish dish served as an appetizer. This dish is prepared by soaking delicate white fish meat, such as red snapper or lemon sole, in lime or lemon juice or sour orange juice with onions and hot peppers.

Brush biscuit tops with milk and sprinkle with sesame seed before baking. The baked biscuits will have a crunchy, toasted top.

SEVILLE ORANGE *(suh vil', sev' il)* — A variety of orange with bitter pulp and peel. Seville oranges are used in making marmalade with an aromatic bitter tang; they are also used in the manufacture of orange-flavored bitters which are used in making mixed drinks. (See also *Orange*.)

SHAD — A food fish related to the herring. These fish grow to a length of 30 inches and a weight of 14 pounds. They have a silvery coloring with a bluish-green tint on the back, and a dark spot and several lighter spots just behind the gills. The shad migrate upstream to spawn (like salmon), then journey to the sea. They are found in the Mediterranean Sea and the Atlantic and Pacific oceans.

Shad has been fished in America for centuries. The American Indians along the eastern coast were using shad for food long before the Europeans discovered America. The Indians' fishing and cooking techniques were picked up by the early settlers and many are still used today.

In colonial times, shad was so plentiful and inexpensive in America that it became known as food of the poor classes. However, the wealthier colonists were unable to resist its fine flavor, and shad soon appeared in menus at parties and dinners attended by early statesmen such as George Washington.

Americans made several attempts to spread the shad to new waters. In the 1870s, shad were successfully planted along the Pacific coast. However, they never flourished in the inland streams and lakes. Today shad is found on the market from January to June. The fish are sold whole, drawn, or in fillets. Upon request, the fish market will remove the bones so the fish will be easier to eat.

Shad can be baked, broiled, boiled, steamed, fried, planked, and stuffed. Whatever method you use, the skin should be left on during cooking to hold the delicate, pink flesh together.

The roe from shad is also considered gourmet fare when it is used in making many appetizers and entrees. It can be purchased fresh or canned.

Shad supplies protein, minerals and B vitamins in the diet. A four-ounce serving of baked shad contains 200 calories, and three and a half ounces of raw roe contains 130 calories. (See also *Fish*.)

SHAKER COOKERY—The cooking techniques and dishes developed by an offshoot Quaker group, called Shakers, in Massachusetts. It is characterized by genuine simplicity and excellent quality.

The Shakers, so named because of a ritual dance, were among English Quakers who fled to the American Colonies seeking freedom to exercise their religious beliefs. They advocated communal living and pacifism. Shakers settled in the northeast, founding a handful of small communities. Even though only a few of these settlements remain today, several museums and restored or preserved villages retain furniture, handwritten recipes, and numerous ingenious cooking or homemaking aids that the Shakers skillfully created.

Because of the philosophy of communal living, the Shaker women cooked for the entire community. To make this as efficient as possible, the Shakers devised a number of ideas for large-scale cooking: piping water to cooking areas; stone sinks; baking and canning kitchens; a type of revolving oven that allowed many pies to be baked together; and baskets and wooden firkins for holding foods.

As much as possible, the Shakers grew their own food, or gathered it from the surrounding woodland. Herbs were grown in abundance, and milk, cream, butter, and lard were favored cooking ingredients. Such sought-after items as lemons, which were valued for many cooking uses, and refined sugar had to be obtained from non-Shaker communities.

Also, because of the Shakers' austerity, they were most particular about not wasting food. They dropped the traditional, rather sloppy method of measuring ingredients by plops, globs, or describing amounts as "walnut- or egg-sized" and established exact weights and measures for their ingredients. They cherished every scrap of food, a philosophy that led to large-scale canning. Any edible portion of food that could be canned was used—for example, the Shakers made apple peel jelly and pickled fruit peel.

The Shaker diet, at one time completely meatless, consisted of many vegetables, fruits, cereals, eggs, cheese, and dairy products. Religious practices prompted a meat ban observed by many Shakers during the 1830s and 1840s.

Baking was an important part of Shaker cookery. Bread was basic, made from flour milled to retain the germ (whole wheat) and homemade yeast. Thus, the daily loaf was often a true wheaten bread. But they turned out other types, including salt-rising bread, potato bread, muffins or gems, tea breads—nearly two dozen kinds in all.

Cakes were made with precisely proportioned and measured ingredients. Maple syrup and sugar, honey, and molasses were used when ordinary sugar was scarce. A plentiful supply of sugar meant delectable pound cakes, sponge cakes and cookies would emerge from the ovens. Rosewater was prepared for use as a flavoring, and herb seeds were used in cookies. Butternuts and hickory nuts, gathered in the woods, supplied a crunchy taste that made layer and loaf cakes special treats.

Shakers baked pies of infinite variety, the crusts plain, buttery rich, or puffy, depending on the filling. There were fruit and berry pies and such favorites as pumpkin, maple custard, and cider syrup pies. Plus, when there was no ban on it, meat pies supplemented the roasts, steaks, chops, hams, and salt pork more commonly used as main dishes. The Shaker cooks also produced a variety of puddings, velvety custards, dumplings of many flavors, and apples gelled in boiled syrup.

The herbs of the garden, fresh in the summer and dried for winter use, were added to many Shaker foods. There was likely to be a touch of rosemary in spinach, savory in beans, a rose geranium leaf in a glass of apple jelly, a sprig of marjoram or thyme in a stew, or a few nasturtium leaves in a lettuce salad. Mixed herbs seasoned the meat dishes.

The Shakers' significant way of living and their pride in workmanship has led to a number of enduring recipes. Excellence in quality and simplicity, along with the overwhelming responsibility women felt toward their families' need for wholesome food, guided the recipe development.

Shaker Baked Beans

Develop rich bean flavor with long, slow cooking—

```
   1 pound dry navy beans (2 cups)
1½ quarts cold water
   1 teaspoon salt
   1 small onion, peeled and sliced
   4 tablespoons butter or margarine
   ¼ cup catsup
   ¼ cup molasses
   1 teaspoon dry mustard
   ½ teaspoon salt
```

Rinse beans; add to cold water. Bring to boiling; simmer 2 minutes. Remove from heat. Cover and let stand for 1 hour. Add 1 teaspoon salt; cover and simmer till beans are tender, about 1 hour. Drain, reserving bean liquid.

Place onion into a 2-quart bean pot or casserole. Add beans. Combine 2¼ cups of the bean liquid with butter or margarine, catsup, molasses, dry mustard, and the ½ teaspoon salt. Pour mixture over beans; cover and bake at 325° for 4 to 4½ hours. Add more liquid to beans, if necessary, during baking. Remove cover last half hour of baking to brown well.

Special Cabbage Salad

```
   4 cups shredded cabbage
½ cup light cream
   2 tablespoons sugar
   1 teaspoon salt
     Dash pepper
   2 tablespoons vinegar
   2 hard-cooked eggs
```

Heap shredded cabbage in bowl. Combine cream, sugar, salt, pepper, and vinegar. Pour over cabbage; toss lightly. Slice eggs; sieve yolks. Arrange egg white rings around rim of bowl; put sieved yolk in center. Serves 6.

Shaker Daily Loaf

```
   1 package active dry yeast
6½ to 7 cups sifted all-purpose
     flour
2½ cups milk
   2 tablespoons butter or margarine
   2 tablespoons sugar
   2 teaspoons salt
```

In mixer bowl combine yeast and 2¾ *cups* of the flour. Heat milk, butter, sugar, and salt just till warm, stirring occasionally to melt butter. Add to dry mixture in bowl. Beat at low speed with electric mixer for ½ minute, scraping sides constantly. Beat 3 minutes at high speed. By hand, stir in enough of remaining flour to make moderately stiff dough.

Let rise in warm place till double, about 1½ hours. Turn out and knead on lightly floured surface till smooth and elastic. Cover and let rest 10 minutes. Shape in 2 loaves. Place in greased 8½x4½x2½-inch loaf dishes. Cover and let rise till double in warm place, about 1¼ hours. Bake at 350° for 35 to 40 minutes.

SHALLOT (*shuh lot'*)—A mild-flavored vegetable related to onions. The bulbs grow in segments, like garlic cloves. At the market shallots resemble small, dried onions with reddish-brown skins having purple-white cloves underneath.

Although several areas on the eastern Mediterranean coast are credited with growing the first shallots, it is known that ancient Greeks obtained this vegetable from the village of Ascalon, Palestine. In fact, shallots, called *echalotes* in French, get their name from this ancient seaport, which is located in the Middle East.

Shallots were first brought into Europe by the French, probably during the first or second century. During the next several centuries the shallot became known and used throughout Europe. In the early sixteenth century, this vegetable was introduced into America, reportedly by followers of the Spanish explorer De Soto.

Fresh shallots should be selected and stored like dry onion varieties. Paper-thin, clean, bright-colored skins and thin-necked, dry, firm bulbs indicate good quality. Shallots are also sold chopped in freeze-dried and frozen forms.

The shallot's segmented structure makes it easy to use a portion of the bulb. Or, you can simply measure out the needed amount of the frozen or freeze-dried forms. Frozen or freeze-dried, shallots substitute equally for chopped, fresh shallots.

Shallots add mellow flavor to any dish in which onions are used. Slice fresh shallots and add them to tossed salads; or dice and cook them in butter, and place them atop broiled steaks. When browning fresh shallots, take care. Overbrowning causes a bitter flavor. (See also *Onion.*)

Barquette of Tiny Shrimp

1½ cups sifted all-purpose flour
½ teaspoon salt
½ cup shortening
4 to 5 tablespoons cold water
1 tablespoon salt
3 cups water
1 pound tiny shrimp in shell *or* 2
    4½-ounce cans shrimp
2 tablespoons finely chopped
    celery
1 tablespoon chopped shallots
½ teaspoon dried dillweed
½ cup catsup
2 tablespoons lemon juice
2 tablespoons mayonnaise
2 teaspoons prepared mustard
1 teaspoon prepared horseradish
    Chopped black olives
    Sieved egg yolk

Sift together flour and salt. Cut in shortening with pastry blender till pieces are size of small peas. Sprinkle *1 tablespoon* of the water over part of mixture. Gently toss with fork; push to one side of bowl. Repeat till all is moistened. Gather up the mixture with fingers; form the dough lightly into a ball.

On lightly floured surface, roll dough to 14x15-inch rectangle. Top with same size aluminum foil; mark in 3x2-inch rectangles. Cut small rectangles with scissors, cutting through pastry and foil at the same time. Turn each rectangle pastry side up; prick well with fork. Moisten 2-inch ends of pastry; pinch together (along with foil) to form "boats," (foil will help keep the shape while baking). Place "boats" on baking sheet; spread sides to keep upright. Bake at 425° till lightly browned, about 10 minutes. Cool. Remove the foil.

Add the salt to water; bring the mixture to boiling. Add shrimp; cover and heat to boiling. Reduce heat; simmer gently till shrimp turn pink, about 5 minutes. Drain. Peel and devein shrimp; chop fine. Combine with remaining ingredients; mix well. Chill. Fill pastry with shrimp; garnish with olives and egg yolk. Serve as appetizer. Makes about 36 appetizers.

SHANDYGAFF (*ṣhan' dē gaf'*) — An English alcoholic drink consisting of ale or beer mixed with ginger beer or ginger ale. The two ingredients are simply mixed by stirring together gently. This cold drink was introduced to India as the beverage to accompany dishes made with curry.

SHANK — A cut of beef, veal, lamb, or pork, taken from the upper part of the front leg. Retail beef cuts include shank cross cuts, while the cuts in lamb and veal are termed fore shanks. In pork, the fore shank is often called hock. Because the shank is less tender than some other cuts, moist cooking methods such as braising and cooking in liquid are recommended.

International outdoor cooking

Feature Lamb Shanks, Armenian-Italian at →
your next outdoor barbecue. Lamb shanks are marinated in an herb-tomato mixture.

Lamb Shanks, Armenian-Italian

 1 cup tomato juice
 ½ cup lemon juice
 ½ cup dill pickle juice
 1 large onion, finely chopped
 1 green pepper, finely chopped
 1 teaspoon salt
 1 teaspoon coarse-cracked pepper
 1 teaspoon cumin
 1 teaspoon dried marjoram leaves,
    crushed
 6 meaty lamb shanks
    Salt

For marinade, combine first 9 ingredients; pour over lamb shanks in deep bowl and let stand 4 hours. Remove from marinade. Salt the meat. Broil over *slow* coals till tender, about 1 hour, brushing with marinade and turning occasionally. Heat the remaining marinade; serve as a relish. Makes 6 servings.

SHAPED COOKIE—A cookie molded by hand from a pliable dough. Roll the dough into a simple ball or form a long, pencil-thin roll and shape into tiny twists of artistry such as candy canes or Christmas wreaths. Select your favorite filling such as dates, candied fruits, or nut pieces around which to wrap a small bit of the cookie dough. Concentrate on keeping the cookies about the same size so they will bake evenly.

Before baking, flatten the cookie balls with the bottom of a glass which has been dipped in sugar or flour. Then use the tines of a fork to make crisscross patterns across the top of the cookie. Or, before baking, press your thumb in the center of the cookie. Fill this indentation with a chocolate piece or a dab of your favorite jelly or jam after baking. (See also *Cookie*.)

Macaroon Bonbons

 2 egg whites
 1 teaspoon vanilla
    Dash salt
 ½ cup sugar
 2 tablespoons all-purpose flour
 1 cup grated coconut
 3 drops red food coloring

Shape cookies into smooth 1-inch balls by rolling between hands. Make a design on cookie by pressing tops with tines of fork.

Beat egg whites with vanilla and salt till soft peaks form. Gradually add sugar, beating to stiff peaks. Fold in flour and coconut. Remove a *third* of dough to second bowl. With food coloring, tint remaining ⅔ of dough pink. Roll pink dough in ½-inch balls; place on greased cookie sheet. With thumb, make small indentation; top with ¼-inch balls of the white dough. Bake at 350° about 8 to 10 minutes. Let stand 1 minute; remove to rack. Makes 30.

Cream Cheese Dainties

 ½ cup butter or margarine
 1 3-ounce package cream cheese,
    softened
 ½ cup sugar
 ¼ teaspoon almond extract
 1 cup sifted all-purpose flour
 2 teaspoons baking powder
 ¼ teaspoon salt
 1½ cups crisp rice cereal, coarsely
    crushed
    Red and green candied cherries

Cream together butter or margarine, cream cheese, sugar, and almond extract till light. Sift together flour, baking powder, and salt; stir into butter mixture just till combined. Chill 1 to 2 hours. Shape into balls; roll in cereal and place on *ungreased* cookie sheet. Top each with a cherry. Bake at 350° for 12 to 15 minutes. Cool on racks. Makes 4 dozen.

Double Buttercups

Press candies in center of each cookie—

Combine 2 sticks piecrust mix, crumbled; one 3-ounce can chow mein noodles, crushed; and ⅓ cup brown sugar. Blend in ¼ cup peanut butter, 1 beaten egg, 2 teaspoons water, and ½ teaspoon vanilla. Shape into 1-inch balls. Place on *ungreased* cookie sheet. Make a large depression in center of each. Bake at 375° for 8 minutes. Using one 11-ounce box bite-sized chocolate-covered peanut buttercup candies (40), press a candy in each center. Bake 2 to 3 minutes. Cool 5 minutes; remove. Makes 40.

Coconut Dainties

    1 cup butter or margarine
    ¼ cup sifted confectioners' sugar
    2 teaspoons vanilla
    1 tablespoon water
    2 cups sifted all-purpose flour
    1 cup chopped pecans

        • • •

    Light cream
    2 cups sifted confectioners'
        sugar
    Tinted Coconut

Thoroughly cream butter or margarine, ¼ cup sifted confectioners' sugar, and vanilla. Stir in water. Add flour and mix well. Stir in nuts.

Shape in 1-inch balls. Bake 1 inch apart on an *ungreased* cookie sheet at 300° till firm to the touch, about 20 minutes. Cool thoroughly before removing from pan.

Add sufficient light cream to 2 cups sifted confectioners' sugar to make of spreading consistency. Dip cookies in icing and roll in Tinted Coconut. Makes 4 dozen.

Tinted Coconut: Shake flaked coconut in covered jar with few drops food coloring.

SHARPENING STONE—A smooth piece of soapstone or a manufactured, shaped carborundum piece used to sharpen knives.

SHASHLIK (*shäsh lik', shäsh' lik*)—The Russian and Turkish name for shish kabob. The marinated meat, usually lamb, is broiled along with vegetables on a skewer.

Lamb Shashlik

Brush melted butter over the skewers of lamb cubes and bright vegetable pieces during broiling—

In deep bowl combine ½ cup olive *or* salad oil; ¼ cup lemon juice; 1 teaspoon salt; 1 teaspoon dried marjoram leaves, crushed; 1 teaspoon dried thyme leaves, crushed; ½ teaspoon pepper; 1 clove garlic, minced; ½ cup chopped onion; and ¼ cup snipped parsley. Mix well.

Cut 2 pounds boneless lamb into 1½-inch cubes. Add lamb to marinade; stir to coat. Cover; refrigerate overnight or let stand at room temperature 2 to 3 hours. Turn occasionally.

Fill skewers, alternating the meat cubes with green pepper and sweet red pepper quarters and thick onion slices. Broil 5 inches from heat till done, about 8 to 10 minutes, brushing frequently with melted butter or margarine. Turn often. Makes 6 servings.

SHEDDAR—The term used for lobsters and crabs whose shells are soft, due to the annual shedding of the old shell and growing of the new one. Blue crabs, commonly sold as soft-shell crabs, and lobster claws that can be broken open with the fingers instead of a nutcracker or similar device are called sheddars.

SHEEPBERRY—A wild berry from the hawthorn shrub. Also called black haw, it is used in jams and jellies. (See also *Berry*.)

SHEEPSHEAD—**1.** A saltwater fish related to the porgy. **2.** Another name for the freshwater drum found in the midwestern and southern United States.

Generally, the saltwater sheepshead lives along the Atlantic, Pacific, and Gulf coasts of the United States. A few of these fish are caught in rivers.

The sheepshead is noted for strong teeth which it uses to crush the shellfish it catches for food. It has a thick body banded with seven or eight dark stripes. The sheepshead can grow as large as 30 inches long and weigh up to 15 pounds. The market size averages 1½ pounds.

The white, tender flesh of this fish has 113 calories in a 3½-ounce serving before it is cooked. (See also *Fish*.)

SHELLFISH

Complete directions on selecting, cleaning, and cooking delicacies from the seas.

A shellfish is a saltwater or freshwater animal with a shell, but no fins, skull, or vertebrae like a fish. Some of the most familiar are the shrimp, lobster, crab, oyster, clam, scallop, and crayfish.

These creatures have been used as a source of food since the beginning of history. Early man undoubtedly found shellfish abundant along the shores and could capture them easily. Then, as he began to migrate, he followed water courses for supplies of food and drink. Even after he settled into an agricultural way of life, man continued to depend on shellfish as a supplement to his daily diet.

He eventually came to consider shellfish as a highly prized delicacy. In Julius Caesar's time, oysters and various forms of shellfish were the first course served at dinners for high state officials. Similarly, the Chinese included shellfish among the 200 or more dishes that were usually served at banquets.

The pilgrims who came to America found the coast teeming with shellfish. They used them as basic food just as the American Indians did. But when the settlers began to move westward, they were too far from the coast to get shellfish.

With the development of modern freezing methods and rapid transportation, Americans throughout the country have been able to obtain fresh shellfish. Since this relatively recent development, shellfish has become universally popular.

Crab and shrimp star in menu

← Plan a dinner around rich shellfish baked in coquilles. A vegetable, salad, white wine, and peaches complement Seafood Bake.

Nutritional value: Shellfish, like fish, are an excellent source of easily digestible protein, minerals, and vitamins. They are particularly rich in the minerals—calcium, phosphorous, iron, copper, magnesium, and iodine. The B vitamins, vitamin A, and vitamin D are also present.

All shellfish are lean and low in salt content, which makes them suitable for low-calorie or low-sodium diets.

In addition to being a very healthful food, they appeal to most palates.

Types of shellfish

The various types of shellfish have a number of common characteristics. Most are hatched from eggs in a form quite different from the adult. They pass through a series of developmental phases before they finally reach adulthood.

Shellfish eat both animal and vegetable matter. Since they do not have to exert much energy to hunt for food, their muscles do not become tough, and they have especially tender meat.

There are basically two types of shellfish—the mollusks and the crustaceans. The mollusks have a soft body partially or completely enclosed in a shell. Those with shells of only one part, such as the abalone, conch, and periwinkle, are univalve mollusks. The clam, cockle, mussel, oyster, and scallop are bivalve mollusks because of their two-part shell.

The crustaceans usually have elongated, segmented bodies with crustlike shells. Their eyes are mounted on movable stalks and their bodies are not always symmetrical. For instance, a pair of claws are sometimes different sizes. Those in this category include the lobster, crab, shrimp, crayfish, and prawn.

Each type of shellfish has individual characteristics and habits which distinguish it from the others in this group.

Abalone: These marine snails are found on the coasts of California, France and South Africa. The large footlike muscle tastes like clam, but needs tenderizing and must be pounded with a mallet. Fresh abalone is available only near the coast. Canned and frozen abalone can be found elsewhere in seafood stores. Because the Chinese-Americans have incorporated abalone into many of the dishes of their cuisine, abalone is also available in many oriental specialty food stores.

Conch: This shellfish with the beautiful spiral shell inhabits southern waters such as the Florida coast, the Caribbean Sea, and the Mediterranean Sea. The large muscle of the conch has a fine flavor, but it must be tenderized before cooking. Conchs are available canned. Many Italian specialty food stores carry them.

Periwinkle: Small marine snails, called periwinkles, are found in salt or fresh water in Europe and on the eastern coast of North America. The muscle has gained much popularity in the British Isles.

Clam: Hard, soft-shell, surf, butter, littleneck, and pismo clams are found along the various coasts of America. Because the clams burrow deeply into the sand and are difficult to harvest, certain species were expensive for many years. In the 1950s, the invention of a hydraulic dredge made harvesting easier. Now more abundant supplies are available to those who enjoy the traditional clambake, clam chowder, and clam entrées.

Cockle: Cockles are found in the salt waters that surround England, France, and America. The sweet meat is eaten raw or cooked like clams. Although cockles have never been a popular dish in America, these small delights are available in American markets canned or shelled.

Mussel: These small shellfish are found in both salt and fresh water, but only those from salt water are eaten. They have long been a favorite in Europe, especially in France. Mussels have not been widely used in the United States even though they are abundant. They are usually cooked with white wine, butter, and shallots.

Oyster: In America most oysters are found along the East and Gulf coasts from Massachusetts to Texas and along the West Coast from Washington to Mexico. The principal types of oysters include the Eastern, Pacific, and Olympia.

Oysters are cultivated underwater with the same attention that truck gardens are given. Oysters are eaten either raw or cooked, and are used in stews, and as appetizers, and entrées.

Scallop: These shellfish are found along the coast from New England to the Gulf and off Alaska. Most Americans eat only the "eye" or large muscle that opens the shell. Europeans, however, eat the entire scallop. The sweet, white, firm meat of scallops is eaten raw or cooked as appetizers, salads, and main dishes.

Crab: The most common types are the king, Dungeness, stone, tanner or snow, and blue crabs, which are found along all United States coasts. Long, coarse fibers make up the crab meat, which is generally tender and sweet. Crab is cooked and eaten hot or cold, either alone or in mixtures. It is used in appetizers, soups, chowders, gumbos, salads, and entrées.

Crayfish: These shellfish quite closely resemble a lobster in appearance and taste. In fact, saltwater varieties, which live along the southern Atlantic, Pacific, and Mediterranean shores, are called spiny or rock lobsters.

Lobster: Northern or Maine lobsters in America are found along the eastern coast from Virginia to Maine. Spiny lobsters are in Florida, southern California, South Africa, Australia, and the Mediterranean.

Lobsters are the largest shellfish and the sweet meat is picked from the shell after cooking, for eating plain or for combining with other ingredients.

Prawn: Prawns resemble large shrimps with which they are frequently confused. They are found in temperate and tropical waters, both fresh and salt. Prawns are used in the same way as are shrimp.

Shrimp: Proclaimed by many as the most popular shellfish, shrimp is enjoyed for its sweet, firm meat. These small, slender shellfish are caught in south Atlantic, Gulf, Maine, California, and Alaskan waters. They are cooked and served hot or cold, either alone, with a sauce, or in combination with other ingredients.

Selection of shellfish

Going to the fish market or supermarket to buy shellfish can be an adventure when you know what you want and how to select the best products. Decide how much will be needed and which form will best fit the recipe preparation—live in the shell, fresh, frozen, or canned.

How much to buy

Shellfish	Amount for 1 person*
Abalone	5 ounces
Clam (in shell)	15 to 20
(shucked)	½ to ¾ cup
Crab, whole blue	2 to 4
whole Dungeness	½ to 1
Crab meat	4 ounces
Crayfish	10
Lobster, whole	1 pound
Lobster meat	4 ounces
Lobster tails	1 tail
	8 ounces
Mussels	12
Oysters (in shell)	6
(shucked)	½ to ¾ cup
Prawns	6 large
Scallops	4 to 5 ounces
Shrimp	6 large
(shelled)	4 ounces

*The amounts listed are average servings as an entrée. If persons are hearty eaters, larger amounts may be needed. When served as an appetizer or with a rich sauce, less is needed.

Fresh: Each type of shellfish can be purchased in a wide variety of fresh forms. Some shellfish are sold alive and the consumer does all the preparation, while others have been shucked or cooked before they are sold at the market.

Those that are marketed alive must be active. Crabs and lobsters should show movement in the legs. Hard clams, oysters, and scallops should close their shells tightly when they are tapped gently. If the shellfish do not show these signs of life, then probably they are dead and should not be purchased or eaten.

Most of the shellfish are available shucked, which means that the scallops, oysters, clams, or mussels have been removed from their shell while alive and then packed in clear liquid. This saves the consumer much time and work.

Shrimp and prawns are usually sold with the heads removed. A greenish or pink color, firm texture, and mild odor are indications that shrimp are fresh.

Lobsters and crabs are also sold cooked. The market cooks the shellfish and sells them whole or the meat is picked from the shell and is packaged and chilled.

Frozen: Shellfish are frozen in practically every form: cooked, uncooked, in the shell, and out of the shell. Some are sold breaded and ready to fry or bake.

Canned: Whole shellfish, lumps of meat, minced meat, and smoked meat are canned for wide distribution. These may be "dry packed" in a vacuum without liquid, or "liquid packed" in a brine or juice.

The federal and state governments have adapted standards to assist the consumer in purchasing shellfish. These standards are reflected in the listing of correct contents and amounts on the label.

The U.S. inspection shield on shellfish indicates that the product was processed under the supervision of a trained government inspector. Shellfish that meet specifications can also be given the Grade A rating just as fish are graded.

Many coastal states have inspection programs to make sure that shellfish are not taken from polluted waters or processed under unsanitary conditions.

Storage of shellfish

Shellfish are quite perishable. They must be carefully handled and refrigerated to preserve quality. Cook live ones immediately and use cooked meat quickly.

For longer storage, freeze fresh and live shellfish. Oysters, clams, and scallops should be shucked before freezing; use within three months. Lobster and crab should be cooked before freezing; use within a month. Freeze uncooked shrimp, in shells or shelled; and keep as long as three months. Thaw shellfish in the refrigerator or cook while frozen.

Commercially frozen shellfish will keep about four months in a home freezer. Canned products will keep a year.

Preparation of shellfish

The most important principle in cooking shellfish is to cook them only until done, for overcooking toughens the meat. Mollusks, such as oysters and clams, are done when the meat curls around the edges or when the shells open, and crustacea, such as lobster and shrimp, are done when they turn a bright pink or red color.

Shellfish are eaten raw, steamed, boiled, broiled, baked, or fried. Each method of cookery should be explored to discover the flavor of shellfish in various forms.

Raw: Oysters, clams, and scallops are the shellfish most commonly eaten raw. Because the muscles are tender and the flavor delicate, they are regarded as gourmet fare. The only preparation necessary is to open the shells (insert knife between halves, pry open, and cut muscle free).

Serve these raw shellfish very cold. Placing one half of the shell and the muscles on a bed of cracked ice keeps them cold and is an attractive way of serving them. Lemon juice, lime juice, freshly ground pepper, or horseradish can be served to accent the flavor as desired.

Boiling or steaming: These methods of cooking shellfish require a short time and minimum preparation. Some shellfish need scrubbing or cleaning, but some clean themselves if placed in salted water.

Shellfish should be alive when put into boiling water or steamed, but you need not worry—the shellfish are killed instantly. With a little practice, one learns to do this quickly and easily.

Plunge the lobsters and crabs into boiling salted water or court bouillon for about 20 minutes. With clams, oysters, and scallops, boil or place them on a rack in a deep pot or kettle with a small amount of boiling water (water does not touch them). In about 5 minutes, the shells open, showing they are cooked. Any shells that do not open with the majority must be discarded. This indicates the shellfish was not alive when cooking began.

Once cooked, serve these shellfish in the shell and let each person pick out the meat for himself. You can remove the meat before serving if you prefer.

Boiled or steamed shellfish meats are frequently combined with ingredients for an entrée, casserole, appetizer, salad, soup, chowder, or sauce. Cook the meat at home, or buy it already cooked in a can or in a package of fresh-cooked meat.

Spinach–Shrimp Salad

  ⅔ cup salad oil
  ⅓ cup orange juice
  2 tablespoons sugar
  1 tablespoon vinegar
  ½ teaspoon grated orange peel
  ¼ teaspoon salt
  ¼ teaspoon dry mustard
    Dash bottled hot pepper sauce
      • • •
  1 large avocado
  1 tablespoon orange juice
  1 pound fresh spinach, torn in pieces (12 cups)
  2 cups cooked, shelled shrimp
  3 oranges, sectioned

In screw-top jar combine salad oil, the ⅓ cup orange juice, sugar, vinegar, orange peel, salt, dry mustard, and hot pepper sauce. Shake well and chill. Makes 1⅓ cups dressing.

Just before serving, peel avocado and slice into rings; sprinkle with orange juice. Combine avocado, spinach, shrimp, and oranges in salad bowl. Toss with dressing. Serves 6 to 8.

Seafood Salad

3 tablespoons lemon juice
2 cups cooked shrimp, crab, *or*
   lobster meat
1 cup chopped celery
   Mayonnaise or salad dressing
3 hard-cooked eggs, sliced
   Lettuce
   Lemon wedges

Sprinkle the 3 tablespoons lemon juice over shellfish. Add celery. Moisten with mayonnaise; season with salt and pepper. Fold in hard-cooked eggs. Arrange salad in lettuce-lined bowl with lemon wedges. Makes 4 to 6 servings.

Crab-Filled Abalone Shell

1 cup cooked crab meat
1 tablespoon diced celery
1 tablespoon mayonnaise
1 teaspoon prepared horseradish
½ teaspoon lemon juice
   Salt
   Pepper
   Abalone shell
   Lettuce

Combine crab meat, celery, mayonnaise, horseradish, and lemon juice. Add salt and pepper to taste. Line an abalone shell with lettuce; fill with the crab salad. Makes 1 serving.

Tossing Spinach-Shrimp Salad with a slightly sweet, orange French dressing brings out the best in all the fresh flavors. Serve this meal-in-one salad for lunch or a light supper.

Split jumbo shrimp about halfway through and stuff with a well-seasoned clam mixture for the unusual Clam-Stuffed Shrimp.

Seafood Soufflé Pie

 1 stick piecrust mix
 2 3-ounce packages lime-flavored gelatin
 ½ teaspoon salt
 2 cups boiling water
 1 cup cold water
 1 cup mayonnaise or salad dressing
 2 tablespoons lemon juice
    . . .
 1½ cups diced, cooked shrimp
 2 cups diced, peeled avocado
 ½ cup diced celery
 2 tablespoons finely chopped onion

Using piecrust mix, prepare and bake one 9-inch pastry shell following package directions. Dissolve gelatin and salt in 2 cups boiling water. Stir in 1 cup cold water, mayonnaise, and lemon juice; beat till smooth. Chill till partially set. Whip till fluffy. Fold in shrimp, avocado, celery, and onion. Chill till mixture mounds when spooned. Pour the shrimp mixture into the baked pastry shell. Chill till firm, about 4 to 5 hours. Garnish with additional whole, cooked shrimp, if desired. Makes 6 servings.

Crab Meat Suzette

Adapted from the famous dessert, Crepes Suzette—

 ⅓ cup sifted all-purpose flour
 1 tablespoon sugar
  Dash salt
 1 egg
 1 egg yolk
 ¾ cup milk
 1 tablespoon butter or margarine, melted
    . . .
 1 tablespoon butter or margarine
 1 tablespoon all-purpose flour
  Dash salt
  Dash white pepper
 ½ cup milk
 1 cup crab meat *or* 1 6-ounce package frozen crab meat, thawed
 1 tablespoon lemon juice
 2 teaspoons dry sherry
  Dash bottled hot pepper sauce
  Dash Worcestershire sauce
 ½ cup hollandaise sauce (See *Hollandaise Sauce*)

Measure the first 7 ingredients into a blender container or a mixing bowl; blend or beat till the batter is smooth.

In a saucepan melt the 1 tablespoon butter over low heat. Blend in the tablespoon flour, dash salt, and white pepper. Add the ½ cup milk all at once; cook quickly, stirring constantly, till mixture is thickened and bubbly. Add crab meat, lemon juice, sherry, hot pepper sauce, and Worcestershire sauce; heat through and keep warm while cooking crepes.

Lightly grease a heavy 6-inch skillet and heat till a drop of water dances on the surface. Lift skillet off heat and pour in 2 tablespoons of the batter. Tilt from side to side till batter covers bottom of skillet evenly. Return skillet to heat and cook till underside is lightly browned, about 1½ minutes. Remove crepe by inverting skillet over paper toweling. Cook remaining crepes the same way, on one side only. Spread 1 tablespoon of the hot crab meat filling across the unbrowned side of each crepe.

Place in a 400° oven and heat till edges of crepes begin to toast. Remove from oven and spoon hollandaise sauce over. Serve as appetizers or entrée. Makes about 11 crepes.

Broiling: All types of shellfish are appropriate for broiling. The direct heat of this method cooks the meat quickly, thus, leaving it moist and tender.

Broiling shellfish expands beyond the kitchen and the range. Other equipment cooks the shellfish in the same manner and moves out-of-doors with the festivities. Cooking on a grill, hibachi, rotisserie, portable appliance, and with kabobs uses the same type heat and techniques.

Shucked mollusks, lobster tails, crab legs, shelled shrimp, and whole shellfish are popular to broil. Whole shellfish must be killed just before broiling. Plunge the shellfish into boiling water for a few minutes or sever the spinal cord. After either method, split open the shellfish and remove the inedible organs. During broiling, brush the meat with melted butter and season with salt and pepper.

Over-the-Coals Lobster Tails

  ⅓ cup salad oil
  ¼ cup sauterne
  ½ cup soy sauce (optional)
  1 small clove garlic, crushed
  ¼ teaspoon ground ginger
  ¼ teaspoon paprika
    Dash pepper
      • • •
  6 frozen lobster tails (about 6
    ounces each), thawed
  3 lemons, halved crosswise

Combine salad oil, sauterne, soy sauce, garlic, ginger, paprika, and pepper. Let stand 1 hour. Cut underside membrane of lobster tails around edges and remove meat from shell. Thread lobster tail lengthwise on skewers alternately with lemon halves. Brush lobster meat with sauce.

Broil, meat side up, over *hot* coals 10 minutes, brushing occasionally with sauce. Turn and broil till lobster is cooked through, about 20 minutes longer, brushing meat occasionally with sauce. Remove from skewers; serve with hot lemon halves. Makes 6 servings.

To cook on rotisserie: Thread lobster tails and lemons on spit. To keep tails from turning, insert skewers parallel to spit, through 2 or 3 tails. Let revolve over *hot* coals 35 to 40 minutes; brush occasionally with sauce.

Scallops à la Jimmy

  1 pound fresh or frozen scallops
  ¼ cup butter or margarine, melted
  ⅓ cup fine soft bread crumbs
  ⅛ teaspoon garlic salt
  ⅛ teaspoon dry mustard
  ⅛ teaspoon paprika
  2 tablespoons dry sherry
    Lemon wedges

Thaw frozen scallops. Slice large scallops in half horizontally. Pour *2 tablespoons* of the butter in a shallow baking pan; arrange scallops in single layer. Combine bread crumbs, garlic salt, dry mustard, paprika, and remaining butter; sprinkle over scallops. Broil 4 inches from heat till lightly browned, 6 to 8 minutes. Drizzle wine over scallops; serve hot with lemon wedges. Serves 6 to 8.

Barbecued Shrimp with Lemon

During the cold months, broil shrimp in the oven and cut the cooking time by a few minutes—

  12 ounces fresh or frozen shelled
    shrimp
  3 large cloves garlic, sliced
  ¼ cup butter or margarine
  ½ lemon, sliced *paper-thin*
    Chopped parsley

Thaw frozen shrimp. Cook garlic in butter 2 or 3 minutes. Line a shallow pan with foil (or use a shallow, foilware pan); arrange shrimp in a layer over bottom. Dash with salt and pepper. Place lemon slices over shrimp. Drizzle with garlic butter; sprinkle with parsley. Cook over *hot* coals till done, about 6 to 8 minutes; turn the shrimp frequently.

Baking: Two forms of shellfish are used in baking—the raw shellfish and cooked meat. The raw form bakes in much the same way as it broils. Butter, lemon juice, sauce, and seasonings are added for flavor.

Shellfish that are eaten raw can be included in a baked dish without previous cooking. Cooked meat is frequently combined with other ingredients and baked for an appetizer entrée, or casserole.

Crab-Swiss Bites

Crisp water chestnuts garnish these delicious, cheesy appetizers—

- 1 7½-ounce can crab meat, drained, flaked, and cartilage removed
- 1 tablespoon sliced green onion
- 4 ounces process Swiss cheese, shredded (1 cup)
- ½ cup mayonnaise or salad dressing
- 1 teaspoon lemon juice
- ¼ teaspoon curry powder

. . .

- 1 package flaky-style refrigerated rolls (12 rolls)
- 1 5-ounce can water chestnuts, drained and sliced

Combine crab meat, green onion, Swiss cheese, mayonnaise or salad dressing, lemon juice, and curry powder. Mix well. Separate rolls; separate each into three layers. Place on *ungreased* baking sheet; spoon crab meat mixture onto rolls. Top each with a few water chestnut slices. Bake at 400° till golden brown, about 10 to 12 minutes. Makes 36 appetizers.

Seafood Bake

Pictured on page 2052—

- 1 10½-ounce can condensed cream of celery soup
- ¼ cup milk
- 1 beaten egg
- 2 tablespoons grated Parmesan cheese

. . .

- 1 7½-ounce can crab meat, drained, flaked, and cartilage removed
- 1 4½-ounce can shrimp, drained
- 1 3-ounce can sliced mushrooms, drained

. . .

- 3 tablespoons fine dry bread crumbs
- 2 tablespoons grated Parmesan cheese
- 1 tablespoon butter or margarine melted
  Parsley
  Lemon twists

Combine cream of celery soup, milk, egg, and the two tablespoons Parmesan cheese in a saucepan. Stir over low heat till cheese is melted and mixture is hot. Stir in crab, shrimp, and mushrooms. Spoon into 4 large baking shells.

Toss dry bread crumbs with 2 tablespoons Parmesan cheese and melted butter. Sprinkle crumbs over the mixture in shells.

Bake the mixture at 375° for about 20 minutes. Garnish each serving with parsley and a lemon twist. Makes 4 servings.

Cassola de Peix

French version of seafood casserole—

- 2 tablespoons butter or margarine
- 2 tablespoons all-purpose flour
- ¼ teaspoon salt
- 1 cup milk
- 12 medium shrimp, cooked and split, or 1 4½-ounce can shrimp
- 1½ cups crab meat *or* 1 7½-ounce can crab meat, drained, flaked, and cartilage removed
- 1 cup steamed lobster *or* 1 5½-ounce can lobster
- 1 3-ounce can sliced mushrooms, drained
- 2 tablespoons dry sherry
- 1 tablespoon lemon juice
  Dash bottled hot pepper sauce
- ¼ teaspoon Worcestershire sauce

. . .

- 2 ounces sharp process American cheese, shredded (½ cup)
- 1 cup soft bread crumbs
- 2 tablespoons butter or margarine, melted

Melt the 2 tablespoons butter over low heat. Blend in flour and salt. Add milk all at once. Cook quickly, stirring constantly, till sauce thickens and bubbles; remove from heat. Add shrimp, crab meat, lobster, mushrooms, sherry, lemon juice, hot pepper sauce, and Worcestershire sauce; mix well. Place mixture in a 1-quart casserole dish. Sprinkle cheese over top. Combine bread crumbs and 2 tablespoons melted butter; sprinkle over cheese. Bake at 375° till heated through, about 40 minutes. If desired. garnish top with mushroom caps and additional seafood. Serves 4 to 6.

Clam-Stuffed Shrimp

1 pound large shrimp in shells
¾ cup rich, round cracker crumbs
3 tablespoons butter, melted
1 7½-ounce can minced clams, drained
2 tablespoons snipped parsley
⅛ teaspoon garlic powder
⅓ cup dry white wine

Shell and devein shrimp. Slit each along vein side about halfway through. Combine crumbs and butter. Stir in clams, parsley, garlic powder, ⅛ teaspoon salt, and dash pepper. Stuff each shrimp with clam mixture. Arrange in an 11¾x7½x1¾-inch baking dish. Bake at 350° for about 18 to 20 minutes; baste occasionally with wine. Makes 4 servings.

Shrimp Saki

1 pound fresh or frozen jumbo shrimp, shelled
Dash salt
Dash pepper
Dash paprika
· · ·
2 tablespoons lemon juice
⅓ cup butter or margarine melted

Split shrimp from back and wash thoroughly under running water; place on a baking sheet. Season with salt and pepper; sprinkle with paprika. Bake at 425° for 8 minutes. Remove from oven and place under broiler for 5 minutes. Combine lemon juice and melted butter or margarine; serve with shrimp. Serves 4 to 6.

Choose Crab Meat Suzette, a variation of crepes suzette, or Cassola de Peix for an experience in elegant dining. Cassola de Peix is garnished with shellfish and mushroom crowns.

Crab-Shrimp Bake

Bake in one casserole or in individual bakers—

        1 cup shelled, cooked shrimp
        1 cup diced celery
    ¼ cup chopped green pepper
        2 tablespoons finely chopped
             onion
        1 7½-ounce can crab meat, drained,
             flaked, and cartilage removed
        1 teaspoon Worcestershire sauce
    ¾ cup mayonnaise or salad dressing
        1 cup soft bread crumbs
        1 tablespoon butter or margarine,
             melted

Cut large shrimp in half lengthwise. Combine shrimp, celery, green pepper, onion, crab meat, ½ teaspoon salt, dash pepper, Worcestershire sauce, and mayonnaise or salad dressing. Turn into 1-quart casserole or individual bakers. Combine crumbs and butter. Sprinkle atop casserole. Bake at 350° till hot, 30 to 35 minutes for casserole, and 20 to 25 minutes for individual bakers. Makes 4 servings.

Frying: Shellfish fry in a matter of minutes. Most shellfish deep-fat fry in 2 to 5 minutes and panfry in 5 to 10 minutes to a delicious crispness.

Prepare for frying by shucking or removing any bits of shell and inedible parts. Then, dip the whole shellfish or chunks of meat in an egg batter and roll in a coating mixture of crumbs and flour, cornmeal, or a commercially prepared, packaged mixture. You also can combine the meat with other ingredients for fritters, croquettes, and other fried dishes.

Serve fried shellfish with a sauce, such as tartar or cocktail sauce, or with lemon juice. (See also *Fish*.)

French Fried Shrimp

        2 pounds fresh or frozen shrimp
             in shells
        1 cup sifted all-purpose flour
    ½ teaspoon sugar
        1 slightly beaten egg
        2 tablespoons salad oil

Thaw frozen shrimp. Combine flour, sugar, egg, salad oil, ½ teaspoon salt, and 1 cup ice water. Beat smooth. Shell shrimp, leaving last section and tail intact. Butterfly shrimp by cutting almost through at center back without severing tail end; remove vein. Dry.

Dip shrimp into batter; fry in deep, hot fat (375°) till golden. Drain. Serve with a cocktail or seafood sauce. Makes 5 servings.

Clams Parmesan

Cheese adds a unique flavor—

    48 large, shucked clams
        2 beaten eggs
        2 tablespoons milk
                 •   •   •
    ½ cup fine saltine cracker crumbs
    ½ cup grated Parmesan cheese
    ½ teaspoon salt
        Dash pepper
        Shortening
        Lemon wedges

Dry clams with paper toweling. Combine beaten eggs and milk. Mix cracker crumbs, Parmesan cheese, salt, and pepper together. Dip clams in egg mixture, then roll in cracker mixture. Panfry on both sides in small amount of hot shortening, about 4 to 5 minutes. Serve with lemon wedges. Makes 4 to 6 servings.

SHEPHERD'S PIE—A hash of chopped meat, vegetables, tomato sauce or gravy, and mashed potatoes. The potatoes can form a cover over the hash or a wall around the edge. Forcing the mashed potatoes through a pastry tube adds an artistic touch.

Shepherd's pie makes very good use of leftover meats and vegetables. Use convenience products for a speedy dish, or substitute for any of the leftovers that may happen to be missing.

Modern version of traditional dish

Serve supper in a hurry by making Shortcut → Shepherd's Pie from frozen vegetables, canned beef, and instant mashed potatoes.

Shepherd's Pie

½ cup finely chopped celery
2 tablespoons chopped onion
2 tablespoons butter or margarine
2 tablespoons all-purpose flour
1 cup milk
¾ cup beef *or* lamb broth
2 cups cooked lamb, cut in cubes
1 tablespoon snipped parsley
½ teaspoon salt
⅛ teaspoon pepper
⅛ teaspoon dried dillweed (optional)
¼ teaspoon Kitchen Bouquet
2 cups seasoned mashed potatoes
¼ cup shredded sharp process
American cheese

In a skillet cook celery and onion in butter till tender but not brown. Blend in flour. Add milk and broth all at once. Cook and stir till mixture thickens and bubbles. Stir in lamb, parsley, salt, pepper, dillweed, and Kitchen Bouquet. Pour meat mixture into a 1½-quart casserole and top evenly with the mashed potatoes. Sprinkle with cheese. Bake at 400° till brown, about 20 to 25 minutes. Serves 6.

Short- cut Shepherd's Pie

1 10-ounce package frozen mixed
    vegetables
1 tablespoon instant minced onion
2 tablespoons butter or margarine
2 tablespoons all-purpose flour
1 14½-ounce can evaporated milk
1 12-ounce can roast beef, cut
    into cubes
    Packaged instant mashed potatoes
    (enough for 4 servings)
2 slices process American cheese

Cook vegetables and onion following package directions; do not drain. Stir in butter. Combine flour and 1 *cup* milk; stir into vegetables. Cook and stir till mixture thickens. Add beef and juices to vegetables; heat to boiling. Turn into 4 casseroles. Prepare potatoes following package directions, *except substitute ⅔ cup evaporated milk for milk called for.* Pile atop meat. Top each with a triangle of cheese. Broil 4 inches from heat for about 3 to 4 minutes. Makes 4 servings.

SHERBET *(shûr′ bit)* — 1. A frozen dessert made with milk and sugar, usually flavored with fruit. Familiar types of sherbets include the fruit-flavored sherbets that are commercially prepared and the kinds that are prepared in the home freezer, some of which may be flavored with wines or liqueurs. 2. A sweetened fruit drink.

Although sherbet, ice cream, and ices are all frozen desserts, they differ somewhat in ingredients. Ice cream is a richer product made with cream, while ices are made with water. Home-frozen sherbets on the other hand, are prepared with milk.

Commercially, sherbet is made with an ice cream mix and acidulated fruit syrup. Stabilizers and emulsifiers are added for uniform body and texture.

Each of the basic ingredients has its own particular function in the preparation of homemade sherbet.

The fruit gives the sherbet mixture its flavor, which generally is tart. Fruit incorporated into sherbets is generally in the form of a purée or a juice.

Milk contributes to the creamy texture of a sherbet. Both the solids and fat in milk help interfere with crystal formation, giving a finer-textured product with many small crystals. Even though sherbets are made with milk, they are considered to be low in fat and milk solids content compared to most frozen dairy products.

Sugar is also an important ingredient in sherbets. Surprisingly, you will find more sugar in sherbet than in ice cream. This is one of the reasons why sherbets are not that much lower in calories. Sugar not only adds sweetness, but it decreases the freezing point of the sherbet mixture. Therefore, it is important that the freezer section of your refrigerator maintain a low temperature in order to keep the sherbet as firmly frozen as possible.

Homemade sherbets are also improved with a stabilizer. Gelatin and marshmallows are two stabilizing ingredients frequently used in recipes. Stabilizers are added to slow down the formation of large crystals, important for a creamy sherbet.

There are two factors in the preparation that are important for a creamy product: the agitation the mixture receives and the temperature used for freezing.

Frequently, recipes call for beating the partially frozen mixture in a bowl, then returning it to the freezer till firm. Beating is preferred when preparing sherbets because the agitation aids in forming small crystals, helps incorporate air, and increases the total volume.

It is also important to freeze the sherbet quickly at low temperatures, for the faster the mixture freezes, the smaller will be the ice crystals that form. The presence of these small ice crystals makes for a smooth creamy sherbet.

Nutritional value: Because sherbets contain milk, they contribute some calcium, phosphorus, the B vitamins thiamine and riboflavin, and some protein and fat.

There are about 130 calories in a half-cup serving of orange sherbet—roughly the same as ice cream. This calorie similarity stems from two main factors—less air is incorporated into sherbet, and the amount of sugar used in the preparation of sherbet is greater than for ice cream.

How to use: Sherbets are one food that can be served as an appetizer, as a main course accompaniment, or as a dessert. For instance, an appetizer fruit cup is often served with a small scoop of a complementary-flavored sherbet. Or, cranberry sherbet occasionally accompanies a turkey or roast beef dinner. But usually sherbet is served for dessert because it is so light and makes the perfect ending for a spicy or particularly filling meal.

Sherbet and Spice

In a bowl stir 1 pint lemon sherbet just to soften. Fold in 1 tablespoon finely chopped candied ginger. Turn sherbet into chilled refrigerator tray. Freeze till firm. Serve with fresh fruit for dessert or appetizer.

Light and luscious dessert

Have Nectarine Sherbet on hand in the freezer for a refreshing hot-weather dessert. Trim with mint and pass nut-topped cookies.

Nectarine Sherbet

 1 envelope unflavored gelatin
   (1 tablespoon)
 1 cup sugar
 ⅛ teaspoon salt
 1¼ cups milk
 1½ pounds fresh nectarines
   (about 6)
 2 tablespoons lemon juice
 1 egg white

In saucepan combine gelatin, sugar, and ⅛ teaspoon salt. Stir in milk. Stir over low heat till gelatin dissolves; cool. Peel, slice, and purée or *very finely chop* nectarines; stir in lemon juice. Stir nectarine mixture into gelatin mixture; mix thoroughly. Add a few drops red food coloring, if desired. Pour into 9x9x2-inch pan or 2 refrigerator trays; cover and freeze till almost firm.

Turn into chilled bowl; add unbeaten egg white. Beat with electric or rotary beater till smooth and fluffy. Return to pan; freeze till firm, 4 hours. Remove from freezer 10 minutes before serving. Trim with mint, if desired.

Lemon juice and peel combine with melted marshmallows to make Lemon Chiffon Sherbet as cool and light tasting as its name.

Pineapple Sherbet

 ½ envelope unflavored gelatin
   (1½ teaspoons)
 2 cups buttermilk *or* sour milk
 ¾ cup sugar
 1 8¾-ounce can crushed
   pineapple
 1 teaspoon vanilla
 1 egg white
 ¼ cup sugar

Soften gelatin in 2 tablespoons cold water; dissolve over hot water. Combine buttermilk, ¾ cup sugar, pineapple, vanilla, and gelatin; mix. Turn into refrigerator tray. Freeze firm.

Break in chunks; turn into chilled bowl. Beat smooth with beater. Beat egg white to soft peaks; gradually add ¼ cup sugar, beating to stiff peaks. Fold into pineapple mixture. Return to *cold* tray. Freeze. Serves 4 to 6.

Lemon Chiffon Sherbet

 2 cups miniature marshmallows
 ¾ cup skim milk
 ½ teaspoon grated lemon peel
 ¼ cup lemon juice
 3 egg whites
 3 tablespoons sugar

In saucepan combine marshmallows and milk; stir over low heat just till marshmallows melt. Remove from heat; stir in lemon peel and juice. Chill till partially set. Beat egg whites and dash salt till soft peaks form. Gradually add sugar, beating to stiff peaks. Fold into marshmallow mixture. Turn into refrigerator tray; freeze till firm. Makes 4 to 6 servings.

Pink Velvet Sherbet

 1 10-ounce package frozen
   strawberries, partially thawed
 1 6-ounce can evaporated milk
 ½ cup sugar
 1 tablespoon lemon juice

Break fruit into chunks. Place all ingredients and 1 cup crushed ice in blender container. Blend at high speed till thick, 2 minutes. Freeze in refrigerator tray. Makes 3 servings.

SHERRY — A blended, amber appetizer or dessert wine with a characteristic nutty flavor. Although sherry is traditionally made from the juice of palomino grapes, today many other grape varieties also are used. And because brandy is added to the grape juice during production, its alcoholic content is often as high as 20 percent.

People have been sipping sherry for centuries. It was first made about 31 B.C. in the region around Jerez de la Frontera in southeastern Spain. But there was no wide recognition of sherry until centuries later when some of the wine was taken to England under the name Vino de Jerez. The English translated this first to jerries, then sherries, and finally, just sherry.

The elegant flavor of sherry has been praised by many notables, including Shakespeare, who said of the amber colored wine: "If I had a thousand sons, the first human principle I would teach them should be to foreswear thin potations and to devote themselves to sherry."

How sherry is produced: Today, sherry production is centered largely in the United States, Spain, South Africa, and Australia. Two methods of production are commonly used. The first, the traditional method, is still used in Spain and in some of the other countries, too. The second, a modern approach to production, is more often used in the wineries in the United States.

The traditional method follows some unique stages of fermentation, aging, and blending. The fully ripe grapes are first picked and laid in the sun to dry slightly, then crushed. At one time, the grapes were placed in wooden troughs and crushed by men wearing specially designed cleated shoes. The dancing movements they used to crush the grapes illustrated the jubilant atmosphere that pervaded the harvest. But due to high labor costs and sanitary considerations, most, if not all, grapes are crushed mechanically today.

Following crushing, the grape juice is transferred to bulk casks called butts where fermentation begins. The lightly covered butts of fermenting juice are often placed out of doors and are subjected to direct sunlight. This technique helps the development of the sherry flavor.

Since no two butts ferment in the same way, an essential element of good wine production is the accurate evaluation of the developing wine by tasters. After the wine has fermented for several months, it is analyzed and divided into two major categories. Judgments are based on flavor, bouquet, and the amount of *flor*, or flower. (*Flor* is the unique yeast that develops on the surface of the sherry.) The wines that are clean, light-bodied, and that have good bouquet and *flor* are destined for the drier sherries, called finos and have brandy added to about 15 percent alcohol. Heavier, fuller-bodied wines with less bouquet and *flor* are labeled oloroso and contain from 16 to 18 percent alcohol. The smaller alcohol content of the finos enables the *flor* to continue developing its unique flavor, while the higher alcoholic content of the oloroso kills the *flor*. Both finos and olorosos rest for a year or two more, during which time they are periodically classified into more specific groups.

At last the wines are admitted to the beginning phases of the solera, a system of blending which enables vintners to maintain a uniform style and quality of sherry from year to year. The solera consists of pyramids of butts, usually about three butts high. Age of the wines progresses from the top of the stack on down.

Again astute tasters are needed to determine how and when the wines in the solera are to be blended. Up to a third of the wine in the bottom cask is drawn off for either bottling or more blending. The amount that has been lost in the bottom butt is then replaced by wine in the middle butt. Likewise, that in the middle is replaced by wine from the top butt and newly fermented wine or wine from a more recent solera is added to the top butt. Thus solera-blended sherry may be a blend of only one or many soleras.

Although a few select sherries are prepared by this method in the United States. most American sherries are blended before fermentation. The grape juice, a blend of varieties, is fermented into a dry white wine; then brandy is added. At this point in the processing, the wine may be made into sherry by the flor method or baked in large tanks at 120 to 140 degrees for about two or three months. This baking replaces sun aging, yet, at the same time, helps to give the same characteristic sherry flavor. The wine is then aged in barrels.

Types of sherry: Sherries are divided into distinct categories according to their relative dryness or sweetness. Spanish-produced sherries often are labeled with the Spanish designations as well as the better-known American names.

Spanish sherries are generally classified as being finos (dry) or olorosos (sweet). Well-known finos, starting with the driest, include manzanilla, fino, and amontillado. From slightly sweet to very sweet olorosos are amoroso, oloroso, cream, and brown sherries. Finos tend to be pale in color with rich flavor and bouquet; olorosos are usually dark and heavier flavored.

Sherry terminology used in the United States has been simplified. A pale, dry sherry is very dry, while a cocktail sherry usually is less dry. Medium, straight, or golden sherry, is not really dry or sweet. Cream sherry, on the other hand, is the sweet dessert wine. Some wines that are marketed as select sherries contain the traditional palomino grapes, which are prepared in the age-old way.

How to use: Sherry is one of the most popular aperitif and cooking wines. Drier sherries are usually designated for appetizer uses, while sweeter sherries are more appropriate for dessert courses.

When sherry is served as a beverage, there are several guidelines that are recommended for the homemaker to follow. It is common, for example, to serve sherry chilled as an appetizer beverage, and at room temperature (60 to 70 degrees) as a dessert. Plan on at least three ounces of sherry for each serving. As an appetizer, chilled sherry in a wine glass or sherry "on the rocks" is superb by itself or served with hors d'oeuvres, nuts, or cheeses. At the dessert course of a meal, serve cream sherry with fresh fruit, cookies, nuts, cheese, or thin slices of fruitcake.

Sherry is also one of the most versatile wines for cooking. Sherry accents dips and soups for the first course. For entrées, it is particularly suitable in poultry, fish, shell-fish, or ham dishes. And for desserts, the flavor of sherry excels in compotes, cakes, and pies. (See also *Wines and Spirits.*)

Marinated Broiled Chicken

½ cup dry sherry
½ cup salad oil
½ cup soy sauce
1 teaspoon ground ginger
⅛ teaspoon garlic powder
. . .
1 2½- to 3-pound ready-to-cook
    broiler-fryer chicken, cut up
1 tablespoon sesame seed

Combine first 5 ingredients. Pour over chicken in flat dish and marinate in refrigerator for 4 hours or overnight. Broil, skin side down, in broiler pan (without rack) 5 to 7 inches from heat till lightly browned, about 20 minutes. Turn; broil 15 to 20 minutes longer. When almost done, brush the chicken with the marinade. Sprinkle with sesame seed; return the chicken to broiler and brown. Makes 4 servings.

Tenderloin Deluxe

1 2-pound beef tenderloin
2 tablespoons butter, softened
. . .
¼ cup chopped green onion
2 tablespoons butter
2 tablespoons soy sauce
1 teaspoon Dijon-style mustard
   Dash freshly ground pepper
¾ cup dry sherry

Remove the surface fat and the connective tissue from meat; spread with 2 tablespoons butter. Place on rack in shallow roasting pan. Insert meat thermometer. Roast at 425° for 20 minutes. Meanwhile, in small saucepan cook green onion in 2 tablespoons butter till tender but not brown. Add soy sauce, mustard, and pepper. Stir in wine; heat the mixture just to boiling. Remove the roast from the oven; pour wine sauce over tenderloin. Return roast to the oven; continue roasting at 425° for 25 to 30 minutes for rare (140°). Baste frequently with sauce. Pass remaining wine sauce with meat. Makes 6 to 8 servings.

Vary shirred eggs with a sprinkling of shredded process cheese. Add cheese the last 5 to 10 minutes of baking just till melted.

Turkey-Ham Casserole

½ cup chopped onion
2 tablespoons butter or margarine
3 tablespoons all-purpose flour
½ teaspoon salt
¼ teaspoon pepper
1 3-ounce can broiled, sliced mushrooms, undrained
1 cup light cream
2 tablespoons dry sherry
. . .
2 cups diced, cooked turkey *or* chicken
1 5-ounce can water chestnuts, drained and sliced
1 cup diced, fully cooked ham
2 ounces Swiss cheese, grated (½ cup)
1½ cups soft bread crumbs
3 tablespoons butter or margarine, melted

Cook onion in 2 tablespoons butter or margarine until tender but not brown. Blend in flour, salt, and pepper. Stir in mushrooms with liquid, cream, and sherry. Cook, stirring constantly, till thickened and bubbly. Add turkey, water chestnuts, and ham. Turn into an 8¼x1¾-inch round ovenware cake dish. Cover with Swiss cheese. Mix bread crumbs with 3 tablespoons melted butter and sprinkle over cheese. Bake at 400° until sauce starts to bubble and top is brown, about 35 minutes. Serves 6.

Sherried-Date Sauce

2 cups pitted dates
¾ cup light corn syrup
½ cup sherry
1 tablespoon chopped, preserved ginger
1 teaspoon shredded orange peel

Cut dates lengthwise in quarters. Combine with remaining ingredients; cover and refrigerate at least 24 hours. Serve the sauce over ice cream. Makes about 2½ cups sauce.

Fruit Refresher

½ cup brown sugar
¼ cup honey
¼ cup dry sherry
2 tablespoons lemon juice
1 teaspoon grated lemon peel
. . .
2 medium unpeeled apples, sliced
2 medium nectarines, peeled and sliced (1½ cups)
2 medium pears, peeled and quartered (1½ cups)
2 medium bananas, peeled and sliced
1 cup dark sweet cherries, halved and pitted

In saucepan combine brown sugar, honey, sherry, lemon juice, and lemon peel. Cook over low heat 5 minutes, stirring occasionally. Remove the mixture from heat and cool.

Combine fresh fruits. Pour dressing over; toss lightly. Cover; chill thoroughly, stirring occasionally. Drain, reserving dressing. Serve fruit on lettuce-lined plates. Pass dressing with salad. Makes 6 to 8 servings.

SHIRR—To bake in a shallow dish till set, usually with reference to eggs. The ramekins, shallow baking dishes, or custard cups that are used should be buttered. Either one or two eggs are added to each dish with a dash of cream and seasonings.

Since eggs are best cooked at a low temperature, place the dishes in a pan of hot water and bake in 325° oven till firm. If soft yolks are preferred, remove the eggs

Marinate chunks of lamb in an herbed mixture. Then, brush Lamb Shish Kabobs with the marinade during broiling.

from the oven when the white is cooked and the yolks quiver when the dish is shaken gently. The eggs will continue to cook as they travel from oven to table.

Variations include a sprinkling of shredded cheese or crumbs over the top of the eggs, or the addition of precooked sausage, ham, or crumbled bacon before the egg is cooked. (See also *Egg*.)

SHISH KABOB, KEBAB (*shish' kuh bob'*) — The Near Eastern name for meat, traditionally lamb or mutton, that is broiled on a skewer. The word shish means skewer, while kabob refers to the small pieces of meat that are roasted. This dish has several names—The Russian refer to it as *shashlik;* the French, *en brochette.*

Shish kabob, or more often just kabob, is now used for any combination of meat and vegetables or just vegetables that are cooked on a skewer. Beef and seafood are incorporated in some versions. Many recipes suggest marinating the meat in a sauce for flavor. (See also *Kabob*.)

Lamb Shish Kabobs

½ cup salad *or* peanut oil
¼ cup lemon juice
1 teaspoon salt
1 teaspoon dried oregano leaves, crushed
½ teaspoon pepper
1 clove garlic, minced
. . .
3 pounds boneless lamb, cut in 2-inch cubes
5 medium onions
4 medium green peppers
3 medium tomatoes, quartered

Combine the first 6 ingredients. Add lamb cubes, stirring to coat. Marinate in refrigerator for 2 days, turning meat several times.

Peel and quarter onions; make each quarter into a cup by removing a few center pieces. Cut the four sides off the green peppers. From each side, carve an oval. On four 12-inch skewers alternately thread pieces of onion, lamb, green pepper, and tomato. Brush kabobs with marinade. Broil 4 inches from heat for 15 minutes. Turn and brush with marinade. Broil 10 minutes longer. Makes 4 servings.

Kau Kau Kabobs

Instant seasoned meat tenderizer
1½ pounds beef round steak, cut in 1½-inch cubes
4 medium green peppers
6 7-ounce frozen lobster tails, thawed and quartered
Preserved kumquats (optional)
. . .
¼ cup sauterne
¼ cup lemon juice
¼ cup salad oil

Use meat tenderizer on meat cubes according to label directions. Cut sides from green peppers and trim to form ovals. Alternate beef, lobster, and green pepper ovals on 4 long or 8 medium skewers. Finish off each skewer with a preserved kumquat, if desired.

Combine sauterne, lemon juice, and salad oil. Broil kabobs over *hot* coals till desired doneness, about 20 minutes, turning often and basting with wine mixture. Makes 4 servings.

Garlic Lamb Kabobs

1½ pounds boneless lamb, cut
    in 1-inch cubes
1 cup garlic salad dressing
    or 1 envelope *dry* garlic
    salad dressing mix*
2 medium green peppers, cut
    in squares
1 16-ounce can small onions

Place meat in shallow dish. Pour dressing over meat. Let stand 2 hours at room temperature or overnight in refrigerator, turning occasionally. Drain meat, reserving liquid. Thread meat and vegetables on skewers in the following order: lamb, green pepper, lamb, onion. Broil 4 inches from heat for about 15 minutes, turning once. Baste meat and vegetables occasionally with dressing. Makes 6 servings.

    *Prepare mix following package directions.

Shish Kabobs Italiano

½ cup Italian salad dressing
¼ cup lemon juice
1 teaspoon dried oregano leaves,
    crushed
2 pounds boneless lamb, cut in
    2-inch cubes

Combine salad dressing, lemon juice, oregano, ¼ teaspoon salt, and ⅛ teaspoon pepper. Place lamb in shallow dish; pour marinade over. Cover; marinate 2 hours at room temperature or in refrigerator overnight, turning meat several times. Thread meat on skewers. Grill over hot coals for 20 to 25 minutes, turning skewers occasionally and brushing with marinade. Makes 5 or 6 servings.

Marinated Beef Cubes

½ cup salad oil
¼ cup vinegar
¼ cup chopped onion
1 teaspoon salt
1 teaspoon coarsely ground pepper
2 teaspoons Worcestershire
    sauce *or* steak sauce
2 pounds beef round steak, cut in
    1½-inch cubes

Combine oil, vinegar, onion, salt, pepper, and Worcestershire sauce. Place beef in shallow dish; pour marinade over. Cover; marinate 2 hours at room temperature or in refrigerator overnight, turning meat several times. Thread on skewers. Broil kabobs over *hot* coals till desired doneness, about 20 minutes. Turn often and baste with marinade. Serves 6.

SHOE PEG CORN—A sweet, white corn with thin, narrow kernels. This type of corn is available either in canned and frozen forms at most supermarkets.

SHOESTRING POTATO—A thin, match-stick size piece of potato that has been deep-fat fried, then salted. Shoestring potatoes are available in packages and various sized cans packed with a vacuum seal, making them easy to keep on the shelf.

    Eat shoestring potatoes by the handfuls or dress them up with a cheese coating. Or, use the potatoes in a casserole to add flavor and texture. (See also *Potato*.)

Parmesan Shoestrings

Empty one 4-ounce can shoestring potatoes into a shallow baking pan. Sprinkle potatoes with ½ cup grated Parmesan cheese. Heat at 350° till potatoes are toasty, about 15 minutes, stirring occasionally. Makes 3 cups.

Tuna Jackstraw Bake

1 4-ounce can shoestring potatoes
1 10½-ounce can condensed cream
    of mushroom soup
1 6½- or 7-ounce can tuna, drained
1 6-ounce can evaporated milk

    . . .

1 3-ounce can sliced mushrooms,
    drained
¼ cup chopped, canned pimiento

Reserve 1 cup of the potatoes. Combine remaining potatoes with soup, tuna, and evaporated milk. Stir in mushrooms and pimiento. Turn into a 1½-quart casserole. Top with reserved potatoes. Bake at 375° till hot, about 25 minutes. Makes 4 to 6 servings.

Trim Scotch Shortbread with gumdrops. Attach decorations with corn syrup.

SHOOFLY PIE — A dessert-type open-face pie that is made with molasses, sugar, and a crumb mixture all baked in a pastry shell. The origin of this pie is credited to the Pennsylvania Dutch homemakers. Some say that it got its name because the flies, attracted to this sweet, molasses dessert, had to be shooed away. (See also *Pennsylvania Dutch Cookery*.)

Shoofly Pie

    1½ cups sifted all-purpose flour
    ½ cup sugar
    ¼ teaspoon baking soda
    ¼ cup butter or margarine
        . . .
    ½ cup light molasses
    ¼ teaspoon baking soda
    ½ cup hot water
        . . .
    1 *unbaked* 8-inch pastry shell
        (See *Pastry*)

Sift together flour, sugar, and ¼ teaspoon soda. Cut in butter till crumbly. Combine molasses, ¼ teaspoon soda, and hot water. Pour ⅓ of liquid in *unbaked* pastry shell; sprinkle with ⅓ of flour mixture. Repeat layers, ending with flour mixture. Bake at 375° about 40 minutes. Cool the pie before serving.

SHORT — A term used to describe a product having a high proportion of shortening. When referring to a pastry or cookie, a short product is rich, tender, and flaky and will break apart or crumble readily. A dough that is short, such as shortcake, has a high proportion of shortening.

SHORTBREAD — A thick, rich cookie made with a high proportion of shortening. Because of the high amount of shortening, usually butter, shortbread is a crumbly type of cookie. The other two ingredients of this Scottish favorite are sugar and flour. Because there are so few ingredients, and because it's easily shaped for baking, shortbread is a very simple cookie to prepare. (See also *Cookie*.)

Scotch Shortbread

    1 cup butter or margarine
    ½ cup sugar
    2½ cups sifted all-purpose flour

Cream butter and sugar till light and fluffy. Stir in flour. Chill several hours. Divide in half. On *ungreased* cookie sheet pat each half into 7-inch circle. With fork, prick each mound deeply to make 16 pie-shaped wedges. (Or on floured surface, roll dough ¼ to ½ inch thick. Cut in 2x½-inch strips or with 1¾-inch cutter.

Bake on *ungreased* cookie sheet at 300° for 30 minutes. Cool slightly; remove from pan. Makes 32 wedges or 42 cookies.

SHORTCAKE — **1.** A dessert or main dish of fruit or a creamed meat mixture served over baking powder biscuits. **2.** The biscuit used for the dessert or main dish. **3.** A cake that is prepared with a large amount of shortening.

Shortcake is a dessert that is as American as apple pie, especially the strawberry version served with whipped cream. Variations are just as popular as the traditional baking powder biscuit-based dessert. Some people prefer sponge cake cups or pound cake for the dessert base. Occasionally, the baking powder biscuits are made with slightly more sugar, egg, or additional shortening to make a sweeter and richer

Springtime favorite

Finish off an all-American Strawberry Short- →
cake, featuring a jumbo baking powder biscuit, with mounds of fluffy whipped cream.

product. The biscuit dough can be baked in one large cake that is split apart for filling, instead of the individual portions familiar to many. Whether the biscuit is buttered or not is also a matter of individual preference.

The toppings, too, can vary just as much as the bases for a shortcake. While strawberries are probably the most popular fruit for the dessert favorite, fresh peaches or other types of in-season fruits and berries are enjoyed. No matter what fruit is chosen, it should be ripe, slightly crushed and sugared, and spooned onto the warm biscuits so that the juices will soak in. Some people prefer a shortcake without the embellishments of cream or ice cream, while others maintain that the shortcake isn't complete if it isn't topped with mounds of whipped cream.

Main dish shortcakes are probably not as familiar as the dessert variety. The base, either a baking powder biscuit, square of corn bread, or split cornmeal muffin, can be topped by creamed meat, seafood, or poultry. (See also *Dessert*.)

Use a serrated knife to split the king-sized biscuit for Strawberry Shortcake. Then, spread the warm bottom layer with butter.

Strawberry Shortcake

    2 cups sifted all-purpose flour
    2 tablespoons sugar
    3 teaspoons baking powder
    ½ teaspoon salt
    ½ cup butter or margarine
    1 beaten egg
    ⅔ cup light cream
      Butter
    1 cup whipping cream
    3 to 4 sugared, sliced
      strawberries

Sift together flour, sugar, baking powder, and salt. Cut in ½ cup butter till mixture resembles coarse crumbs. Combine egg and cream; add all at once, stirring just enough to moisten.

Spread dough in a greased 8x1½-inch round baking pan, building up edges slightly. Bake at 450° for 15 to 18 minutes. Remove from pan; cool on rack for about 5 minutes.

Split in two layers. Lift top off carefully. Butter bottom layer. Whip the cream. Spoon berries and whipped cream between layers and over top. Serve the shortcake warm.

Peach Shortcakes

    2 cups sifted all-purpose flour
    1 tablespoon sugar
    3 teaspoons baking powder
    ½ teaspoon salt
    6 tablespoons butter or margarine
    1 beaten egg
    ⅔ cup milk
    1 quart fresh, sliced peaches
      Lemon juice
      Granulated sugar
    1 cup whipping cream
    2 tablespoons brown sugar
      Butter

Sift together flour, 1 tablespoon sugar, baking powder, and salt. Cut in 6 tablespoons butter till mixture resembles coarse crumbs. Combine egg and milk; add all at once, stirring just enough to moisten. Turn dough out on floured surface; knead gently about 30 seconds. Pat or roll to ½-inch thickness. With floured 2½-inch cutter, cut out 6 biscuits. Bake on *ungreased* baking sheet at 450° about 10 minutes.

Meanwhile, dip sliced peaches in lemon juice to prevent them from darkening. Add granulated sugar to desired sweetness. Whip cream with brown sugar. Fold *half* the peaches into *half* the whipped cream. Split shortcakes in half, and butter bottom layers. Spread peaches and cream mixture on bottom layers of biscuits. Cover top half of biscuit with remaining peaches and cream. Makes 6 servings.